MATT AND TOM OLDFIELD

CLASSIC
FOOTBALL HEROES

CARRAGHER

FROM THE PLAYGROUND
TO THE PITCH

DINO

Published by Dino Books
an imprint of John Blake Publishing
3 Bramber Court, 2 Bramber Road,
London W14 9PB, England

www.johnblakepublishing.co.uk

www.facebook.com/johnblakebooks 🖪
twitter.com/jblakebooks 🖪

This edition published in 2017

ISBN: 978 1 78606 463 9

British Library Cataloguing-in-Publication Data:

A catalogue record for this book is available from the British Library.

Design by www.envydesign.co.uk

Printed and bound in Great Britain by Clays Ltd, St Ives plc

1 3 5 7 9 10 8 6 4 2

Papers used by John Blake Publishing are natural, recyclable products made from
wood grown in sustainable forests. The manufacturing processes conform to the
environmental regulations of the country of origin.

Every attempt has been made to contact the relevant copyright-holders, but some
were unobtainable. We would be grateful if the appropriate people could contact us.

John Blake Publishing is an imprint of Bonnier Publishing.
www.bonnierpublishing.co.uk

For Noah and Nico,
Southampton's future strikeforce

CLASSIC
FOOTBALL HEROES

Matt Oldfield is an accomplished writer and the editor-in-chief
of football review site Of Pitch & Page. Tom Oldfield is a freelance
sports writer and the author of biographies on Cristiano Ronaldo,
Arsène Wenger and Rafael Nadal.

Cover illustration by Dan Leydon.
To learn more about Dan visit danleydon.com
To purchase his artwork visit etsy.com/shop/footynews
Or just follow him on Twitter @danleydon

TABLE OF CONTENTS

ACKNOWLEDGEMENTS

First of all, I'd like to thank John Blake Publishing –
and particularly my editor James Hodgkinson – for
giving me the opportunity to work on these books
and for supporting me throughout. Writing stories for
the next generation of football fans is both an honour
and a pleasure.

I wouldn't be doing this if it wasn't for Tom. I
owe him so much·and I'm very grateful for his belief
in me as an author. I feel like Robin setting out on a
solo career after a great partnership with Batman. I
hope I do him (Tom, not Batman) justice with these
new books.

Next up, I want to thank my friends for keeping

me sane during long hours in front of the laptop.
Pang, Will, Mills, Doug, John, Charlie – the laughs
and the cups of coffee are always appreciated.

I've already thanked my brother but I'm also very
grateful to the rest of my family, especially Melissa,
Noah and of course Mum and Dad. To my parents, I
owe my biggest passions: football and books. They're
a real inspiration for everything I do.

Finally, I couldn't have done this without Iona's
encouragement and understanding during long,
work-filled weekends. Much love to you.

CHAPTER 1

GOODBYE, ANFIELD

19 May 2013
He puts his body on the line for the good of the
team. His passion stood him out from the rest.
He's Bootle's finest and today is his 737th and final
appearance for Liverpool. He's the ultimate one-club
man. Ladies and gentlemen, please put your hands
together for JAMIE CARRAGHER!

The Anfield crowd was cheering so loudly that he
could barely hear the announcer saying his name.
This was it – the big goodbye. Jamie took a deep
breath and walked out of the tunnel and onto the
pitch for the last time. It was nice to have his two
children at his side: son James wore a matching

Liverpool shirt with '23 CARRAGHER' on the back, while daughter Mia wore a red and white dress.

The Liverpool and QPR players stood on either side, forming a guard of honour for him to walk down. As Jamie walked along, he clapped the Liverpool fans on each side of the stadium. Playing for Liverpool wouldn't mean half as much if it wasn't for the club's amazing supporters.

We All Dream of a Team of Carraghers,
A Team of Carraghers,
A Team of Carraghers!

Jamie would never get tired of hearing 40,000 people singing his song. The advertising boards around the pitch all read '23 CARRAGHER, TRUE LEGEND'. The fans held up red and white cards that between them formed 'JC 23'.

'Defenders don't often get this much attention!' he smiled to himself.

Jamie had always known that his final match would be emotional but he still wasn't prepared for this. For twenty-five years, he had given everything for Liverpool Football Club. But in ninety minutes' time, it would all be over. Jamie was determined to make the most of his last appearance. With Steven Gerrard out of the squad due to injury, he had the captain's armband.

'I'd have let you wear it today even if I was playing too!' Stevie told his great friend as he presented him with a special trophy. 'I'm sorry not to be playing on your big day but I'll be out there in spirit.'

Jamie and Stevie had won so many battles together with their spirit and determination. They never gave up and the Liverpool fans loved their local heroes for that.

'If you're not careful, it'll be your big day soon too!' Jamie joked, pointing at the sling around Stevie's left arm.

At thirty-five years old, Jamie no longer had the pace to chase after quick strikers but his voice was still as loud and commanding as ever.

'Mark up!' he shouted to his centre-back partner Martin Škrtel.

'Get back!' he shouted to his midfielders Jordan Henderson and Lucas Leiva.

'What a goal!' he shouted to Philippe Coutinho when he gave Liverpool the lead in the first half.

Jamie was relieved. There was only one way that he wanted to end his Liverpool career – with a win and yet another clean sheet.

For sixty-two minutes, Jamie did what he did best. He organised his teammates, keeping them focused and alert. He read the game brilliantly, spotting any danger and making blocks and interceptions. He wasn't letting anyone get past him on his big day.

Then, in the sixty-third minute, Jamie did something he hardly ever did. When the ball came to him, he was at least 30 yards away from the QPR goal but he decided to shoot. In that second, Jamie became a striker again, for the first time since he was sixteen years old. He struck it beautifully and the ball sailed towards the top corner... the goalkeeper was beaten... but it hit the post!

As Jamie ran back to defence, he cursed his bad luck. 'So close, what a farewell that would have been!'

With ten minutes to go, Jamie was substituted. The score was still 1-0 but his final victory and clean sheet looked safe.

'Well done, Carra!' Jordan cheered as they shook hands.

The whole of Anfield rose to their feet to clap Jamie as he left the field, including the QPR fans. He didn't want to leave the field but, after a last verse of 'You'll Never Walk Alone', it was time to say goodbye.

As a teenager, Jamie had been one of England's top prospects but no-one could have predicted the level of his success. He had never been the most talented footballer in the world but his amazing attitude and work-rate had taken him all the way to the top. No matter which position his managers asked him to play in – centre-back, right-back, left-back, midfield, or attack – Jamie always gave 110 per cent for the team.

The young Everton fan had become a Liverpool player, and now a Liverpool legend. Jamie had won thirty-eight England caps, two FA Cups, three League Cups, the UEFA Cup and, of course, the Champions League. There were so many amazing memories that

he would never forget – including that incredible
night in Istanbul with Stevie, and the FA Cup victory
over Arsenal with Michael Owen.

Jamie had so many people to thank – teammates,
coaches, friends and, of course, family. He couldn't
have achieved his dreams without his mum's
support, or his dad's coaching. Then there were
his wife Nicola and their children, James and Mia.
He would really miss playing football but retirement
would give him more time to spend with his
loved ones.

Jamie's final thanks went to his hometown, the
source of his determination, spirit and courage. He
would always be so proud of where he came from.

'Not bad for a Bootle Boy!' his dad Philly teased
him as Jamie gave one last wave to Anfield.

CHAPTER 2

BOOTLE BOY

'James Lee Duncan Carragher, where do you think you're going?' Paula called from the kitchen, rolling her eyes. It was happening again.

James had seen the sunshine pouring in through the open front door and he wanted to explore. He ran towards the light as fast as his little legs would let him but his mum won the race and scooped him up into her arms. 'Not so fast, little guy! The road is no place for a three-year-old.'

As she held her son in the air, his little legs were still kicking.

'Philly, we have to keep that front door closed

at all times now,' Paula told her husband. 'If I take my eye off James for one second, he's on the move again!'

Philly and Paula smiled at each other. After all their son's early health problems, it was just great to see him moving. Before James was born, the doctors had warned them that their son might have a serious problem with his spinal cord. There was a real chance that he might never be able to walk. Paula, however, refused to give up.

'Trust me, our baby is going to be fine,' she told Philly, proudly stroking her belly.

In the end, Paula was correct but only after some worrying times. There were no problems with James' spine but there were other health issues that the doctors needed to deal with. After an operation and six tough weeks in hospital, their first child was finally fit enough to go home.

'What did I tell you?' Paula smiled happily as they carried James into the car. 'He's a battler. I knew that our baby was special!'

Philly looked down at his son's tiny face in the car

seat and nodded. 'Yes, I reckon we've got a future Everton player here!'

Football was the family passion and the Carraghers were Everton through and through. Philly hardly ever missed a home game at Goodison Park. James' first name came from his grandad but his middle names were a tribute to his dad's favourite Everton legends: Gordon Lee and Duncan McKenzie. Philly's dream was for one of his kids to play for the club.

Paula laughed. 'One step at a time!'

Three years on and they were finding it hard to keep up with James' quick steps. Luckily, the Carraghers lived in a tight-knit community, where everyone knew and helped each other. Plus, James' grandparents lived nearby and they were always happy to help with the babysitting.

Their hometown, Bootle, had a bad reputation for poverty and crime but the people always stuck together. The local pub, The Chaucer, was often their meeting place and Philly Carragher was usually one of their leaders. The tough Bootle spirit was something to be proud of.

'If you can make it here, you can make it anywhere,' Philly liked to say.

By the time James' younger brothers Paul and John were born, the family lived in one of the biggest houses on Knowsley Road. They weren't rich but there was always a bit of extra money to spend on holidays and other nice treats.

'Look! A perfect fit,' Philly cheered when James tried on his first proper Everton shirt.

Paula clapped and then took a photo for the family album. The shirt was far too big for James but she didn't want to spoil her husband's special moment. 'Besides, he'll grow into it,' she thought to herself.

'Philly, I need to pick up some milk from the shop,' Paula called into the living room. He was watching football on TV. 'You need to keep an eye on James while I'm out, okay?'

'Sure,' Philly replied, without turning away from the screen.

The front door slammed shut but moments later, he heard a thud and then a loud crying sound. Philly jumped up out of his chair and rushed into the hallway. James was sitting at the bottom of the stairs. His face was red and wet with tears.

'What happened, kiddo?' Philly asked but the only answer he got was more crying.

As he hugged his son and stroked his hair, he found the bump. It was growing quickly. 'Did you fall and hit your head, little man?'

James nodded and rubbed his eyes.

'You'll be alright,' Philly reassured him. 'You've got too much energy to stay indoors all day. If your mum says yes, you're coming to watch Merton Villa with me next weekend!'

CHAPTER 3

MERTON VILLA PART I

'Come on, Villa, they're walking all over us. Get some tackles in!' Philly shouted angrily from the touchline, moving his arms around quickly to point in lots of different directions.

James stood next to him, watching and learning. For five days a week, his dad was a builder but, at the weekends, he was a football manager. He loved it so much that he coached two teams: The Brunswick and Merton Villa. Philly took his job very seriously and so did James. He was the manager's young assistant after all.

'They're not playing well today, lad,' Philly

muttered. 'I reckon a few of them went out partying last night.'

As James looked out on the Sunday League pitch, there were so many sights to see. There was the patchy green grass that became a mud bath around each goalmouth and corner flag. There were the massive white goalposts with lots of holes in the netting. There were the spectators on the sidelines, including a man with a scary-looking bulldog. There was James' dad and the other team's coach, calling out instructions and biting their fingernails nervously. There was the poor old referee, who the players kept screaming at:

'Ref, how did you miss that? It was the clearest penalty ever!'

And then there were the players themselves. Some were small with big bellies and they seemed to do a lot more shouting than moving. Others were tall and skinny with bright, colourful boots and they fell over a lot, even if the defender didn't touch them. The players came in all shapes and sizes but they had two things in common: they loved football and they loved their team. James already loved the idea of being part of a team. It looked like fun, even when the players weren't smiling.

As the half-time whistle went, the Merton Villa players walked off together, talking about the game. This was the moment that James had been waiting for. As Philly began his big team-talk, James took a football and dribbled onto the pitch. The large ball was difficult for him to kick and it took ages to reach the penalty area. When he eventually got there, the goal looked huge in front of him.

'Surely I can't miss!' James thought to himself. The target was massive. If the Merton players could score goals, then he could too.

He took a long run-up and booted the ball as hard as he could. It didn't go very far and when it landed, the ball slowed right down and then trickled wide. James looked behind him. Luckily, everyone was listening to his dad. No-one had seen his embarrassing strike.

James had time for a few more shots before the teams came back on. Two of them hit the target but a tortoise could have crossed the goal-line quicker.

'Okay, I've got a lot of practising to do,' he said to himself.

By the middle of the second half, James was bored and cold. He wanted to be playing football, not watching it. The game was still 0-0 and there had hardly been any goalscoring chances. He tapped the ball from side to side and waited for the end.

'James, I need your help,' Philly called out. He had thought of a way to keep his son interested. 'I'm going to bring on Kev up front but should I take off Neil or Paddy?'

James didn't know who either of them was, so he just picked a name. 'Paddy.'

His dad nodded. 'Good call. Paddy it is.'

James watched as a big, powerful man came on and a smaller, skinnier man came off. He was pleased with his decision.

In the last minute, Merton won a corner and all their tallest players ran into the penalty area. James could hear the arguments going on in the box. He was learning lots of new words but he wasn't sure that his mum would let him use them at home.

'Come on, Villa!' Philly shouted.

The cross flew right into the danger zone and, eventually, Kev managed to scramble the ball into the net. 1-0 to Merton! The whole team went wild and so did Philly on the touchline. He pumped his fists and lifted James high into the air.

'What a substitution, kiddo!' he screamed. 'And did you see who took that corner?'

James shrugged. In all the excitement, he was a bit confused.

'It was Neil, the guy you told me to leave on the field. You're a genius!'

James smiled proudly. He had helped his dad's team to win the game.

'Do you fancy coming again next week?' Philly asked him on the way home. 'We need you!'

James nodded happily.

'Great!' Philly said, ruffling his son's hair. 'It was a poor performance today but, in the end, that doesn't really matter. Winning – that's all that matters!'

James sat next to him, listening and learning.

CHAPTER 4

EVERTON'S BIGGEST FANS

'Mum, look!' James shouted, pointing at the TV screen. 'That's Dad!'

Paula rushed into the living room and stared in horror. Her son was right; that was definitely Philly.

'Oh what's he up to now?' she groaned.

Her husband had run onto the pitch at Wembley and he was dancing crazily with the Everton players.

'Mum, don't be too mad,' James said with a big smile on his face. 'We just won the FA Cup!'

Just as his dad had always hoped, James was already a big Everton fan. And after watching Philly's joy at Wembley, he begged his dad to let him go to the games too.

'I'm six years old now!' James argued. 'I promise I won't get bored. Please! Please!'

'Okay but if you need the toilet, you'll have to wait until half-time or full-time. I'm not missing any of the action!' When it came to Everton, his dad could never say no.

James' first trip to Goodison Park came at the start of the 1984–85 season, when he was six years old. Wearing his latest Everton shirt, he had never been so excited. As they turned the street corner, there it was, rising up above the houses: Goodison Park.

'It's beautiful!' James cried out, staring up at the size of it.

His dad laughed. 'I've never heard anyone call it that before!'

James' smile only got bigger as they went through the turnstiles and up into the stands. The atmosphere inside was absolutely amazing. The 30,000 fans stood and sang song after song together at the tops of their voices. It was a million times better than watching Merton Villa. Before kick-off, he went up on his dad's shoulders to get a better view of the pitch.

'Dad, which one is Graeme Sharp?' James asked. From up in the stands, the Everton players were a long way away and they all looked very similar in their blue shirts and white shorts.

'He's the Number 9,' Philly replied. 'That's him warming up the goalkeeper!'

As they watched, 'Sharpy' thundered a shot into the top corner of the net. James cheered and thought back to his own shots at Merton Villa. He had a very long way to go if he wanted to be as good as his hero.

James was desperate to see Everton win. He hadn't even thought about them losing but their opponents Tottenham were a brilliant team. Glenn Hoddle, Clive Allen and Gary Mabbutt were all England internationals and Ossie Ardiles played for Argentina. In the end, Everton lost the match 4-1. It wasn't a great Goodison Park debut for James.

'Sorry son, I hope that didn't put you off coming again?' Philly asked as they walked home.

James shook his head fiercely. 'Not at all, I loved it!'

His dad laughed. 'That's the spirit! There are lots of ups and downs in the life of an Everton fan. But if you start with the lows, it can only get better!'

Luckily for James, it got a lot better very quickly. Soon Everton were winning match after match and he saw them all. If it was a home match, they were there in the crowd at Goodison Park. If it was an away match, they would listen anxiously to the radio for score updates.

And whether it was home or away, there was always *Match of the Day*. His dad recorded the TV show every week and James watched the Everton games again and again, until he knew the commentator's words off by heart.

'Sharp has got past the Watford defence... and past Coton in goal. It's Watford 3 Everton 5!'

James wanted to know everything about football. *Shoot!* magazine was the best place to find out about his favourite players. Every Saturday morning, he would wait impatiently for it to arrive. One week, it even came with a big Graeme Sharp poster. He pulled it out and put it straight up on the wall above his bed.

'Good night, Sharpy!' James liked to say before he went to sleep.

Everton weren't just top of the league; they were also doing well in the FA Cup and the European Cup Winners' Cup. No team had beaten them for months. Paul and John had now joined the Everton supporters' club too. Their mum bought them all matching blue 'EFC' jumpers, and took way too many family photos.

But only James was old enough to go to the matches with his dad. That made him feel very special.

'Son, this is an historic season for us!' Philly said excitedly. 'I think it's time for you to come on a few away trips with me.'

In the European Cup Winners' Cup semi-final, Everton faced German giants Bayern Munich. The first leg was away in Germany and James was there in the Olympiastadion with his dad, cheering on their team. The game finished 0-0 but there was no such thing as a boring football match. James had the best time of his life. After the match, one of the Everton players stopped the team bus and handed him a can of coke.

'Don't open it,' Philly joked. 'That'll be worth a fortune one day!'

Even better was still to come. Back at Goodison

Park, in the second leg, James screamed with joy as Everton beat Bayern 3-1. Then, in the final, they beat Rapid Vienna by the same score.

'I can't believe it!' Philly cheered. 'Do you remember that awful first match of the season against Tottenham? Look at us now.'

James nodded, jumping up and down on the sofa. 'We've won the double!'

'And we've still got the FA Cup Final to come, kiddo. We could win the treble!'

After the last FA Cup Final, there was no way that James was staying at home this time. When it came to Everton, his dad could never say no.

As they travelled down to Wembley, James didn't feel too nervous about the match. He wanted Everton to win, of course, but they had already won the First Division title and the European Cup Winners' Cup. For once, he wasn't too disappointed when his team lost to Manchester United.

'What a season!' Philly said on the way home.

James smiled. He couldn't wait to start playing club football like his Everton heroes.

CHAPTER 5

MERTON VILLA PART II

'How old are you, lad?' Peter Halsall, the manager, asked him.

'Eight,' James lied, trying to look tall and sound confident. He was only seven but he would do anything to join Merton Villa. 'And I'm a really good striker!'

Peter looked at the small, skinny boy in front of him. Was Philly's son telling the truth about his age? He couldn't be sure but he didn't want to upset an eager kid. In the end, Peter just smiled and shook James' hand. 'Great, welcome to the club!'

James was delighted as he ran over to join the other boys for their dribbling drills. Wearing his favourite Everton shirt, he was on his way to becoming the next Graeme Sharp. As he joined the back of the line, however, the smile left his face. This was serious football now. During the training session, he worked really hard to impress his new coach.

'Nice work, James!' Peter called out as he weaved through the cones as quickly as he could. The ball only touched one along the way.

After a few minutes, James' face was bright red and soaked with sweat but he was having the time of his life. He was making new friends already. He loved being part of a team, just like the older Merton Villa players that he used to watch by his dad's side.

In the match at the end of the session, James took up his favourite position in attack. He felt that he had done well so far but this was his biggest challenge. As soon as the game started, he chased after the defenders like an angry bull. He didn't let them have any time on the ball.

'He's certainly not a lazy striker!' Peter thought to himself on the touchline. The kid was clearly very determined.

Soon, one of the defenders made a mistake and
James pounced. As he dribbled into the penalty area,
he looked up and picked his spot. Where would
Sharpy aim for? Bottom right corner. James waited
for the keeper to rush out and then placed his shot
carefully, with just enough power.

*Goooooooooooooooooooooooaaaaaaaaaaaaalllllllll
lllllllllllllllll!!!!!!!!!!!!!!!!!!!*

James didn't celebrate. This was only practice; he
would have plenty more goals to celebrate in Merton
Villa's proper league matches.

Philly came to collect him at the end of training.
'How did he get on?' he asked Peter. James was
standing next to him, waiting nervously for the
answer.

The youth coach laughed. 'He's definitely your
son! You worked your socks off today, lad. Well done.
If you play like that every week, you'll be a star!'

James' face lit up and his dad gave his hair a firm
ruffle. 'That's my boy!'

Only a few months later, James was picked to play
for the Merton Villa Under-11s. A lot of the other

boys were three years older than him but he wasn't scared. He was tougher than he looked and he was the best young striker at the club. He loved to win, and as his dad had taught him, winning was the most important thing.

'Get the ball to me and I'll score!' he told his teammates confidently.

Nothing could stop James, except really, really bad weather. In the car on the way to one game, he looked out of the window and groaned. It wasn't just drizzling; it was raining heavily. By the time they arrived at the ground, it had turned into a big hailstorm. The stones were nearly as big as golf balls.

James looked across at his dad as if to say, 'Really, I have to play football in *that* weather?' but Philly just opened the car door and got out. James counted to three and then raced into the changing room, where it was warm and dry. He could tell by looking at his teammates' faces that they didn't want to play either.

The hailstorm continued but the referee didn't call the match off. As he went out to warm up, James' shirt was soaked right through to the skin.

'This is awful!' he complained to his mate Charlie, but he just nodded and shivered. They had no choice but to play.

As the match kicked off, James had an idea. If he was injured, he wouldn't have to play! So when the first defender tackled him, he fell to the floor holding his leg.

'Owwwwwwwwwwwwwww!' he cried out, trying to make his pain look as realistic as possible.

James may have fooled the referee but he didn't fool his dad. Philly stormed onto the pitch and walked him straight back to the car. On the drive home, they sat in total silence, except for the rain hammering against the windows. James knew that he was in big, big trouble.

He went straight to his room and waited for his dad's punishment. Eventually, Philly walked in. He still looked furious.

'There are no excuses for what you did today,' he began.

'But Dad, it was–' James pleaded.

'No excuses! You let your coach down, you let

your teammates down, you let me down and you let yourself down. No son of mine takes the easy way out when things get tough. You're a Bootle boy and next time, you're going to show it. Do I make myself clear?'

James nodded, looking down at the floor. He wished that his dad would just leave him alone.

'Do I make myself clear?' Philly repeated.

'Yes, Dad,' James said quietly.

At the time, he was angry and upset but once he had calmed down, James felt ashamed. His dad was right; he had let everyone down. He had learned an important lesson. If he wanted to become a top footballer like his Everton heroes, he couldn't just walk away when he felt like it. He had to be brave and determined at all times, no matter what.

A few hours later, James crept downstairs. He found Philly watching TV in the living room.

'I'm sorry,' James told him, looking down at the floor. 'That won't happen again, I promise.'

His dad nodded. 'I'm glad to hear it. Now, come and watch the football with me.'

CHAPTER 6

FAMILY FUN

'Sharpy dribbles towards the defender. He fakes to go left but he goes right instead. He's left the defender behind and now he only has the goalkeeper to beat. He hits it low and hard… and it's in! *Goooooooooooo aaaaaaaaaaaalllllllllllllllllllllllllllllllll!!!!!!!!!!!!!!!!!!!!!!*'

James ran towards the imaginary Everton fans and jumped into the air with his arms out wide. His brother John, 'the goalkeeper', chased after the ball, which had gone deep into the bramble bushes. His other brother Paul, 'the defender', sat down grumpily on the grass.

'I'm bored, can't we play a different game?' Paul asked. 'A game where we *all* get to have fun?'

James thought for a minute. He didn't mind playing something else but it had to be something that he would be the best at. He was very competitive. What could they do? Despite his best coaching, his brothers weren't very good at keepie-uppies yet...

'I've got a new game,' James announced when John returned with the ball. He looked around the park for the right object. 'Okay, whoever can hit that bin first from over here is the winner.'

John nodded but Paul wasn't happy. 'That's not fair – our kick isn't as powerful as yours!'

'Fine, we'll have three different starting points. John, you can go first from up here.'

The youngest brother took a big run-up and toe-punted the ball towards the target. It travelled quite far but in a completely different direction to the bin.

'Unlucky!' James shouted as John jogged off to get the ball back.

It was Paul's turn next and he was taking it very seriously. He placed the ball carefully and looked up several times to judge the direction and distance.

James used to be his hero but now he was big enough to challenge his older brother. The days of wanting to wear matching outfits were over. Paul was desperate to beat his big brother at everything. It didn't matter whether it was a game of pool at the pub or kicking a football at a bin in the park. He always wanted to win. He was a Carragher, after all.

But as Paul went to kick the ball, James made a sudden noise to put him off. 'Raaa!'

Paul completely sliced his kick and James fell to the floor laughing. Paul, however, wasn't laughing at all. He was furious. He turned around and jumped on his brother.

'Why did you do that?' Paul screamed, swinging his fists.

'I'm sorry! I'm sorry!' James replied, protecting his face from the blows. His brother was getting stronger all the time.

Fortunately for him, he soon had a lucky escape.

'Boys, lunchtime!' their nan called from across the street.

Suddenly, Paul was more hungry than angry.

Sunday roast was his favourite meal of the week.
He wouldn't miss it for anything. All three brothers
sprinted to the front door.

'Slow down lads, you'll need to wash your hands
before you sit down at my dinner table,' their nan
told them.

There was always plenty of food at the Carragher
family get-togethers. Chicken, potatoes, stuffing,
parsnips and other vegetables, all covered in delicious
gravy. If it was up to James, he would have eaten a
roast breakfast, lunch and dinner.

'Nan, this is your best one yet!' he said happily.
'Can I please have seconds?'

'Of course you can, love,' Ellen replied. 'Just make
sure you leave a little for the rest of us!'

James thought that his brother had forgotten about
his mean trick earlier. After lunch, they all moved
into the living room for some tea and biscuits in front
of the TV. James had a favourite chair and he headed
straight for it. But as he went to sit down, Paul
barged him out of the way and stole the seat.

James couldn't believe it. He stood over his

younger brother, shouting 'Move!' again and again. He was the one getting angry now.

But Paul just shook his head and made himself comfortable.

'Come on boys, no fighting here,' their mum told them, giving them a sharp look.

'Mum, you know that's my chair,' James complained. 'I got there first!'

Paula rolled her eyes and sighed. 'Son, there are plenty of other chairs in the room. Be a good boy and let your brother sit in that one today.'

James stormed over to a seat in the corner and sat there eating biscuit after biscuit in silence. But soon, he was laughing along with the rest of the family as they watched the afternoon comedy shows on TV. James loved Sunday family time. It was the same routine with the same people every week – football, then food, then TV. But when something was that good, why would you want to change it?

James and Paul's fights never lasted long. By the time the family drove back home to Knowsley Road, they were friends again.

'James, do you reckon Everton can reach the FA Cup Final again this season?'

'I don't know, that would be four years in a row!'

'And Gary Lineker's left us to go to Barcelona…'

'Yes, but we've still got Sharpy and Kevin Sheedy. Dad, what do you think?'

Philly always had the last word in the family football debates. 'I think we need to get back to Wembley to wipe the smug look off those Liverpool faces. We have to get revenge for last year's defeat!'

CHAPTER 7

SCOUTED

'Smile for the camera, boys,' the photographer called out. 'James, lift that trophy a little higher so that we can see it clearly!'

St James Primary School had just won the double – the local Division One title and the McDonald Cup. John Rourke, the proud headteacher and coach, had organised a big photo session to celebrate. He wanted everyone to know about his team's success.

The players entered the assembly hall in their full kits – blue shirts, white shorts and blue socks. Like James, John was a huge Everton fan. He even had a season ticket for Goodison Park. The only thing missing from the photo was the football boots.

'Apparently the studs would ruin the wooden floor,' John explained.

The taller boys stood on the back row and the smaller boys sat on chairs in the front row. James wasn't one of the smallest boys but he needed to be at the front for another reason. He was the team captain and he had the McDonald Cup in his hands. Winning the final and lifting the trophy had been the proudest moment of his life so far.

The boys were a bit shy in front of the camera but John was enjoying himself. 'Okay, lads. Now, on the count of three, everyone shout "St James!".'

1, 2, 3, ST JAMES!

Thanks to James' great performances for his school, he had been picked to play for Bootle Boys. It was a big honour because Bootle Boys selected the very best players from all of the schools in the area. And just like at Merton Villa, James was playing against older boys.

'I'm not worried about you, kid,' the Bootle Boys manager Ian Chapman told him with a smile. 'To be honest, I'm more worried about the defenders who play against you!'

James wasn't scared of anything. He was focused on goals and he would do anything to score them. Some of his teammates were more skilful footballers but no-one was more determined than James. He never gave up, no matter what the challenge was. If a centre-back tried to push him around, he stood his ground and pushed back. If a centre-back tried to wind him up with insults, he had a few of his own up his sleeve. James was a Bootle boy, after all.

'Less talk, more action!' Ian shouted from the sidelines if it ever looked like James was letting his battle get in the way of scoring goals.

That rarely happened, however. James finished the Under-11s season as the team's top scorer and he was only nine years old.

'You're unstoppable,' Ian told him after the final match. 'If I had eleven players with your attitude, we would be the best team in the whole country!'

James' coach wasn't the only one who was impressed. Harry Hodges was a scout at Liverpool and he was always looking out for the best new talent in Merseyside. He found plenty of talent in the Bootle Boys team.

One day, Ian asked five of the players to stay behind after practice, including James. 'First of all, I want to say well done this season. You've all been fantastic. And secondly, I've got some amazing news for you. A Liverpool scout has been watching you and he wants you all to go and train at their School of Excellence!'

The other boys were over the moon but James had mixed feelings. It was great that a scout from a top club thought he could be a future star, but he supported Everton, Liverpool's biggest rivals. What would his dad say?

When James told him, he was surprised by Philly's reaction. 'That's brilliant news, son!' his dad shouted. 'Congratulations, when's your first training session?'

'But it's Liverpool!' James reminded his dad. 'I can't go and play for Liverpool... can I?'

'Of course you can!' Philly said. 'We can't always pick who we play for and, although I really hate to say this, Liverpool is a great club.'

James felt better after hearing that. This was a great opportunity for him and he would do everything he could to impress the coaches at Liverpool's School of Excellence.

'If I play really well, maybe an Everton scout will come and steal me away!' James joked with his brothers.

'And then you could tell them to sign me and John too,' Paul continued the dream. 'Three Carragher brothers playing in the same team!'

When the big day arrived, James stood by the front door ready to go. When his dad saw what he was wearing, he frowned.

'Are you sure about that?' Philly asked, pointing at the blue Everton shirt that his son was wearing. 'They're not going to like it at Liverpool!'

'I'm an Everton fan, Dad,' James said. 'If Liverpool want to sign me, they'll have to deal with that.'

It didn't take long for the coaches to notice him.

'Here comes a brave boy!' Hugh McAuley joked with Dave Shannon.

'Yeah, "Sharpy" better be a brilliant player!'

Shannon replied. 'Shall we get him to wear a bib to cover up that awful shirt?'

James loved it at Liverpool. The facilities were amazing, the coaches were friendly and the sessions were fun but challenging. 'Sharpy' was improving all the time and sometimes, the first-team manager, Kenny Dalglish, came down to watch.

For the first time, James started to think seriously about football. Could he really make it as a professional player? He played with technically better players at Liverpool but James was a winner and that was really important. He just needed to keep believing in himself.

One day, James was playing pool with Paul at The Chaucer pub when he overheard one of the locals talking to his dad.

'So is your eldest lad any good at football?' the man asked.

Philly didn't even pause to think about his answer. 'Yes, James will play in the top division in England,' he replied, as if that was a fact.

CHAPTER 8

NO "I" IN TEAM

'How are you doing, lad?' Steve Heighway, the Head of the Liverpool Academy, asked as James arrived for training.

'Fine,' James replied with a small nod of the head. He wasn't in the mood for talking.

Steve patted him on the back but didn't ask any more questions. His office door would always be open if James felt like talking another day.

James' parents had just separated. It could be a very difficult and confusing time and Steve didn't want one of his ten-year-old boys to feel like he had to bottle things up. The Liverpool Academy cared about how their youngsters were getting on, both on and off the pitch. It was important for them to know that it was okay to talk about their feelings.

But James wasn't really thinking about his parents. The strange thing was that not much had really changed. He still lived with his mum and brothers, and his dad still took him to football and watched his matches. They even still went to their nan's house for Sunday roasts. The only difference was that Philly now lived somewhere else.

Instead of thinking about family, James thought about football. That was easy because he was playing more matches than ever, for Merton Villa, Bootle Boys *and* Liverpool. If he ever had an evening off, he went to the Brunswick Social Club, nicknamed 'the Brunny', and played more football with his mates.

'Don't you ever get bored of playing football?' his mum asked him one night at dinner. She couldn't imagine wanting to do the same thing over and over again, every single day.

'Yes, sometimes we play pool at The Brunny instead!'

Thanks to Philly, James had always been

competitive but as he began to take football even more seriously, he became even more competitive. That was both a good thing and a bad thing. He scored even more goals than before but he also lost his temper more often, with referees, opponents and even his own teammates.

James knew how good he was and he expected everyone else around him to be just as good, and just as determined to win. If they weren't, he was very happy to tell them what they were doing wrong:

'What kind of a pass was that?'

'Stop pretending you're Maradona and get the ball up to me!'

'Wake up lads! I can't do this on my own.'

James' comments helped some of his teammates to play better but others really didn't like playing with him. For them, football was meant to be a fun kickaround, not a life-or-death situation. James could sometimes be a cruel bully if they were losing, and sometimes even if they were winning.

When James scored a goal for Bootle Boys in his first game at Anfield, he ran off and celebrated on his own. He believed that he was the best and everyone else was just there to make up the numbers. Every time a pass or cross didn't reach him, James threw his arms up in the air, stamped his feet, and shouted.

Watching from the stands, Steve Heighway was impressed by the boy's performance, but he wasn't impressed by his attitude at all. When they met at the final whistle, it was time for him to teach James an important lesson about teamwork.

'No-one is ever too big for the team,' Steve reminded him. 'Yes, you scored a goal today but did you do it on your own? No, you had ten other players out there helping you. Never forget that, lad. I didn't like what I saw from you out there today. You must always respect your teammates, okay?'

James looked down at the grass and nodded. After thinking about his behaviour, he realised that the Head of Liverpool's Academy was right. He was so obsessed with winning that he wasn't thinking about other people's feelings. That wasn't fair and it didn't help the team. It was time for James to change his style a little. He needed to find a way to stay aggressive on the pitch, but not *that* aggressive. He didn't want his teammates to hate him.

In the next game, when someone played a bad pass to him, he didn't moan or shout at all. And when he scored a goal, he ran to thank his teammate who had set him up.

'Great assist!' he cheered, giving him a high-five.

Everyone noticed the difference in James. 'Are you feeling alright?' Ian, the Bootle Boys manager, asked him at the end of the game. 'Have you lost your voice or something?'

James didn't stay calm and friendly on the pitch for long but his attitude was much better than it had been. Thanks to Steve, he had learnt that anger and shouting weren't the best way to win a football match. Teamwork and determination were much more important.

In the Under-13s local league, Merton Villa lost the title race to their big rivals, Pacific. James was very disappointed but the two teams met again in the Sunday League Cup Final a few weeks later. James couldn't wait for the rematch.

'We can't lose to those lads again,' he told his teammates in the dressing room before kick-off. He had never been so pumped up for a game before. 'It's time for revenge!'

Pacific had a very good team, including Bootle's other best young footballer – a talented midfielder called Jamie Cassidy. Off the pitch, the two were friends but on it, they were enemies. James would never settle for second best; he had to be the top dog. But he couldn't get there on his own. He needed his teammates to help him.

The Cup Final turned out to be a nine-goal thriller. Merton took the lead but Pacific equalised and then took the lead themselves. James never gave up or started moaning. Instead, he kept encouraging his teammates:

'Keep going, we can do this!'

Merton fought back to win 5-4. At the final whistle, James and his teammates celebrated as if they had won the World Cup. They formed a big team huddle and bounced up and down. The victory meant so much to them all. It was the proudest day of their lives.

'Well done everyone!' James shouted. He had scored two of the goals but it had been a great team effort.

That's what James loved most about football – a team winning together.

CHAPTER 9

LEAVING LIVERPOOL

James loved being part of the Liverpool Academy but he was still hoping that one day, his beloved Everton would come along and take him back where he belonged. He wore red when Steve told him to, but he was blue at heart.

'Dad, couldn't you speak to someone at the club?' James asked.

Philly shook his head. 'Look son, I know we love Everton but you've got to think about the football. Now that Howard Kendall has gone, Everton are down in mid-table and who are at the top? Liverpool! You're developing your skills at the best club in the country. Do you know how many kids would kill for that chance?'

James knew that he was very fortunate but that didn't stop him dreaming. One day, he wanted to wear Sharpy's blue Number 9 shirt and listen to the Goodison Park crowd singing his name:

Carra! Carra! Carra!

At the age of eleven, James finally got his opportunity. When Ray Hall, the Head of Everton's School of Excellence, heard that one of Liverpool's top young stars was a big Everton fan, he had to check him out. After watching James play a couple of times, Ray went to speak to him and his dad.

'Well played today!' he said after introducing himself. 'I hear that you're a Toffee. Is that true?'

James nodded eagerly. He knew Everton fans were called Toffees and didn't mind a bit.

'Great, we're always looking for our next star striker! How would you feel about coming down for a trial with us?'

James looked up at his dad with pleading eyes.

'Thanks for the offer but we'll need to discuss it

first,' Philly told Ray. 'If you give me your phone number, I'll give you a call tomorrow.'

The discussions began on the car journey home.

'Please, Dad! I want to go!'

'Are you sure?'

'Yes, because it's Everton!'

'But why do you want to leave Liverpool?'

'Because it's Everton!'

His mum tried too but neither of them could change James' mind.

'Okay, it's your decision,' Philly said eventually. 'If you're determined to leave Liverpool, we're not going to stop you.'

The coaches were sad to see James go but they understood. 'If it doesn't work out at Everton,' Steve told him, 'you'll always have a home here at Liverpool.'

James was very grateful for all their support but he couldn't wait for his Everton trial to begin. This time, he would wear his blue shirt and no-one would say anything about it. Finally, he would fit in properly. Now he was really following in the footsteps of his heroes.

'Welcome to Everton!' Ray said with a big smile, shaking James' hand. 'I've got a present for you.'

Ray handed James a pair of club kit shorts. 'Guess whose these are?'

'Sharpy's?' James hoped. He was *really* excited now.

'Oh no, is he your favourite player? Your mum told me it was Tony Cottee! Sorry, these are his shorts.'

It was still a great gift and James thanked Ray politely. He had already changed into his football kit, so he handed the shorts to his dad. Then he ran out onto the field to join the other players. This was it, the big moment that he had been waiting for. James Carragher was ready to start his incredible Everton career.

Everyone did their best to make him feel welcome at the club but somehow things never felt quite right. At first, everything just felt different. The club had different coaches, different ideas and different training drills. James did his best to adapt and enjoy the Everton way.

'Don't drop so deep! Wait for the midfielders to get the ball up to you.'

'Nice touches, lad, but we want you in the penalty area scoring goals!'

'Jump, win the header and flick it on. Keep it simple!'

However, after a few months, James realised that Everton wasn't just different from Liverpool; it simply wasn't as good. He didn't like to admit it but he had made the wrong decision.

'Fun practice?' his dad asked him as he got into the car.

James decided to tell him the truth. 'Not really,' he replied.

When they stopped at a red light, Philly looked over at his son. He didn't look happy at all. 'What's wrong?'

James took a deep breath and swallowed his pride. 'Dad, I miss Liverpool. Everything was so much better there – the coaching, the pitches, the players, the tactics!'

'I told you so!' was what Philly wanted to say but he didn't. Instead, he tried to help his son. 'Well, Steve did say that you would always be welcome back there. Do you want me to speak to him?'

James nodded. 'Yes please.'

He was very relieved when Steve agreed to let him re-join Liverpool. Arriving at the Liverpool Academy felt like returning home.

'Hello, stranger!' Steve joked. 'Sorry, we've got a new star striker now, so you'll be starting on the bench.'

How had they replaced him already? James' face fell. 'Really?' he asked.

Steve burst out laughing. 'No, but we don't make life easy for traitors!'

James smiled. He loved a tough battle and, this time, he was at Liverpool to stay, no matter what.

CHAPTER 10

LOVING LIVERPOOL

'Jamie, you're not John Barnes, okay? Stop trying to dribble round every single player and cross it into me!' James teased Jamie Cassidy. After playing against each other in the big Merton Villa vs Pacific clashes, they were now Liverpool teammates.

'Oh what, but you're Kenny Dalglish?' David Thompson asked James with a laugh. They had known each other for years, ever since they started playing together for Bootle Boys.

Jamie was always ready with a quick response. 'At least I can win a header, Thommo! You couldn't even outjump my nan, little man!'

It was good to be back at Liverpool. James had forgotten how much fun he had with his friends, both on and off the pitch. Winning was the best feeling in the world and, with the three of them in the team, they won almost every match.

Thommo got the ball in midfield and played it wide to Jamie. He beat the first defender easily and was about to take on the second but then James' voice popped into his head: 'Cross it into me!' He looked up and his teammate was waiting in the penalty area. When the ball arrived, James slid in to tap the ball into the net.

Goooooooooooooooooooaaaaaaaaaaaaaaaaalllllllllllll llllllllllllllll!!!!!!!!!!!!!!!!!!

'Hurray! You listened to me for once,' James joked as they celebrated together. 'Finally!'

'That was just a one-off to keep you quiet,' Jamie replied with a cheeky smile. 'Next time, I'll try some more skills. You lazy strikers can create your own goals!'

People at the club were talking about the three of them as the future of Liverpool but James tried not to get too excited. He still had a long way to go and he hadn't even signed a proper contract yet. As his fourteenth birthday got closer and closer, James began to worry.

'What if they don't want to keep me?' he asked his dad.

'Don't worry – there's no chance of that,' Philly reassured him. His son was going to play in the top division of England. He was absolutely certain about that.

Since James' return to Liverpool, Steve had been keeping a very close eye on his development. He was delighted to see James getting better and better in every area – skill, intelligence, attitude. The club had a very talented group of young players but he was certainly one of the best.

'James needs to sign his schoolboy forms,' Steve told his staff. 'We definitely don't want him to leave us again!'

Walking into Anfield to sign his first Liverpool contract was the best moment of James' life. He had worked so hard to get this far and he hoped that it was just the start of even greater things. If everything went according to plan, he could be playing in the first team in four years.

'Congratulations, lad,' Steve said, giving him a firm handshake. 'I'm glad you came back! You've really earned that deal with all your hard work.'

James' proud parents were there by his side as he put his signature down on the paper. He didn't usually enjoy writing but this was different. He was becoming a proper Liverpool player.

'Soon the fans will be queuing up for that autograph!' Philly laughed. His son was on his way to becoming a professional footballer. Their dream was coming true, even if James would not be playing for Everton.

Steve hoped that the contract would keep James at Liverpool for years but a few months later, James had another difficult decision to make. After weeks of very competitive trials, he was one of just sixteen youngsters selected to go to Lilleshall, the FA's School of Excellence.

'Well done, lad!' his dad said when they found out the good news. 'My boy's going to the national football academy! There's no better place for you.

James wasn't so sure about that, however. It was a real honour to be picked for the final squad but he was developing well at Liverpool. Did he really have to leave the club again? Last time, it had been a disaster. What if he hated the coaches at Lilleshall, or got homesick? The school was a long way from all his friends and family.

Steve had mixed emotions too. 'I'm pleased for you but I'm gutted for me,' he told James. 'I believe that you're the best fourteen-year-old in the country and I don't want someone else coaching you at Lilleshall. I want to coach you here at Liverpool.'

James kept changing his mind. He couldn't decide on the right thing to do. Should he stay with Steve at Liverpool or should he go to Lilleshall? In the end, he decided to go to Lilleshall. It would only be for two years and then he would return to Liverpool.

Two years away from home, where he could play football every day on the best pitches in England – that sounded amazing to James. Plus, Jamie, his Liverpool teammate, would be there too. They were going to have the time of their lives.

CHAPTER 11

THE TWO JAMIES AT LILLESHALL

'How many times have I told you, kid?' the coach asked, rolling his eyes. 'You can't keep swearing like that!'

James swore under his breath this time and then apologised. 'Sorry, I didn't mean it!'

The coach just shrugged his shoulders. All he said was, 'Off you go.'

James sighed and ran over to the corner flag to start another lap of the pitch. If he didn't stop swearing soon, he would be too tired to play football at all!

Apart from the extra running, James was really enjoying his time at Lilleshall. When their bus arrived at the gates on the first day, he couldn't believe it.

'Is this really our home for the next two years?' he asked Jamie. 'This is crazy!'

Lilleshall was a totally different world from Bootle. The bus moved slowly down the longest driveway that James had ever seen. There were big, beautiful gardens and ponds on either side of the path.

'Look!' Jamie shouted, pointing at the perfect green pitches in the distance. 'That's where we'll be playing football every day!'

All of the boys were really excited by the time the bus eventually stopped in front of a large old house.

'Wow, who lives in a place like this?' they asked as they got out and looked up at all the windows and chimneys.

'You all live here now. Welcome to Lilleshall!' one of their new coaches announced, spreading his arms wide.

The tour started with their dorms in the massive mansion. James and Jamie were happy because they got to share a room together. Once they had dropped off their bags, they went on a long walk to visit the incredible football facilities.

'This is the best boarding school ever!' James declared happily.

They had to go to lessons every morning but every afternoon, the boys played lots of football. The coaches had a different style to Steve Heighway at the Liverpool Academy but they were just as good. The other young players were excellent and James was learning lots. He was so glad that he had agreed to go to Lilleshall. It was the best decision of his life.

James wasn't the tallest or most skilful player in the squad but no-one played with more spirit. Even if he didn't score a goal, he made sure that he gave the defenders a difficult time. He chased after every ball and flew into every tackle. Big, powerful opponents never scared him. After all, he was a Bootle Boy.

'How are you, son?' his mum asked on the phone each week. 'We miss you!'

'I miss you too,' James always replied but it was only half-true. It was strange not to see his friends and family all the time, but he was having too much fun to feel homesick.

Towards the end of his first year, James played

a match for Lilleshall against Liverpool at Anfield. James and Jamie couldn't wait to return and show what they had learned. Steve was there to greet them when they arrived.

'The two Jamies are back!' he teased them with a big smile on his face. 'It's time to see what rubbish that posh place has taught you.'

He was always 'James' when he was at home with his family, but when it came to football, he had now become 'Jamie'. The coaches at Liverpool found it easier to talk about 'the two Jamies' who were away at Lilleshall. Luckily, he was happy with the change. 'Jamie Carragher' sounded more like a footballer's name.

Despite all of the talk before kick-off, Jamie didn't play very well in the game. Steve was worried about his best young player but Jamie wasn't. It was just one bad match. He was definitely becoming a better player at Lilleshall.

'Just you wait until I come back next year,' he told Steve. 'Then you'll see my improvement!'

Jamie wasn't picked for the England schoolboys'

team but Lilleshall often represented the country at Under-16 level. Their manager, Keith Blunt, was a big fan of Jamie's energy and attitude.

'Your role tonight is simple,' Keith told him before his debut against Italy. 'I want you to cause as much trouble as possible up front and then if you get a chance to score, score!'

Jamie nodded; that was always his game-plan. As they waited for kick-off, he looked down at the three lions on his white England shirt. He was about to become an international footballer.

'Come on lads, let's make our country proud!' Jamie shouted.

The Italian defence was strong but he never gave up. Eventually, a scoring chance came to him. Jamie stayed calm and aimed for the bottom corner. His shot was so accurate that the goalkeeper, Gianluigi Buffon, had no chance of stopping it.

Goooooooooooooooooooooooooaaaaaaaaaaaaaaaaaa aalllllllllllllllllllllllllll!!!!!!!!!!

Jamie punched the air and ran over to celebrate with his teammates. No matter how good his

opponents were, he couldn't stop scoring. After
that goal, both Jamies were picked to play at the
UEFA European Under-16 Championship in Ireland.
Playing against top countries like Portugal and
Czechoslovakia was a great experience.

Then, after two amazing years, it was finally time
for Jamie to leave Lilleshall. His parents dressed up
and came down from Bootle for the big graduation
ceremony. They clapped and cheered as Jamie went
up on stage to collect his cap.

'Well done, lad!' Philly said, giving him a hug. 'I
hope you haven't got used to this lifestyle, though.
Moving back to Bootle is going to be a bit of a shock
for you!'

Jamie laughed. He had loved his time at Lilleshall
but he was looking forward to his Anfield return. He
was sixteen now and if everything went according
to plan, the Liverpool first team was only a few more
years of hard work away.

CHAPTER 12

CHANGING POSITIONS

Jamie had grown up dreaming of being a striker. He loved scoring goals and he was good at it. But was he good enough to be a Liverpool striker? Ian Rush had scored over two hundred goals for the club and their new young striker, Robbie Fowler, looked like he might score even more. Robbie wasn't very tall but he was really fast and he had an amazing shot.

For the first time in his life, Jamie was having doubts about his ability. After Lilleshall, he was full of confidence about his talent and his future. Back at Liverpool, he had expected to progress through the youth teams quickly. However, it wasn't quite working out that way. Life in the Liverpool 'B' team was tough for a sixteen-year-old. Jamie was playing against big, powerful players and suddenly, football wasn't so easy.

'Get up, kid!' a defender leaned over and shouted in his face. As Jamie picked himself up off the ground, the defender laughed. 'You're going to learn a lot about *real* football today!'

Jamie was still quite small for his age and he wasn't very strong either. He was really determined to win and he never stopped running, but that wasn't enough anymore. He needed to have something special.

'Keep your head up,' Steve Heighway told him. 'Every level is a step up and you're going to need time to adapt. Just be patient, you've got plenty of time! I know you, Jamie. I know you're going to work and work until you reach the top.'

Slowly, Jamie grew taller and started to add muscle to his skinny frame. He learned to be clever and make the most of his skills. Defenders stopped pushing him around as much and he started scoring goals again. The Liverpool coaches were pleased, and promoted Jamie to the 'A' team.

'On to the next step!' he told himself happily.

But Steve was wrong about one thing. Moving from 'B' to 'A' wasn't a step up; it was a leap, and it would be very demanding. Jamie was substituted at half-time on his debut because he couldn't keep up with the pace of the game.

'How am I ever going to be ready for the first-team?!' he thought to himself as he collapsed down on the bench.

But Jamie never gave up on his dream and Liverpool never gave up on him. He did extra training to improve his stamina and by the end of the season, he was one of the team's best players. The coaches decided that Jamie was ready for his next challenge: the Liverpool reserves.

'Congratulations, you're only one step away from the first team now!' his dad Philly reminded him.

Jamie knew that he was getting really close now. He was improving with every game, and it was mostly thanks to one big change. After ten years up front, Jamie's days as a striker were over.

At first, he was very disappointed when they moved

him back into midfield. He had never even thought about playing in a different position. But after speaking with Steve, Jamie felt happier about the switch.

'This happens all the time,' the head of the Liverpool Academy reassured him. 'Trust me, it's a good thing not a bad thing. We know your strengths and we want you to fulfil your potential. Being a striker isn't that great, anyway!'

As long as he was playing, Jamie decided that he didn't mind where he played. It didn't take long for him to feel comfortable in central midfield. In fact, everything seemed to click into place.

'I'm better here,' he told his brothers. 'I'm not quick enough to play up front but I can pass the ball well and I can win the midfield battles all day long!'

There was one other big reason for Jamie's switch. The Liverpool youth team had a new superstar – a speedy striker called Michael Owen. After his two years at Lilleshall, he was back at Anfield and scoring lots and lots of goals.

'He's broken every schoolboy record in the country!' Jamie told his dad.

There was no way that Jamie could compete with Michael up front. So instead, he joined his mates Thommo and the other Jamie in a brilliant and fearless midfield.

'Now I can keep a closer eye on you two,' Jamie joked. 'And I can look after Little Thommo if he gets in any more fights!'

Jamie had always been a leader but now it was easier for him to organise the team from the centre of the pitch. Plus, he could really get stuck into the action.

'Beware of the Bootle Boys!' they chanted with evil grins on their faces.

Soon, the other teams hated playing against Liverpool.

CHAPTER 13

YOUTH CUP WINNERS

The FA Youth Cup was the biggest Under-18s competition in English football. But despite being one of the most successful clubs in the country, Liverpool had never won it. Jamie was determined to change that and make history.

'We've got everything we need to succeed,' he told his teammates. 'Goals, skills, organisation and character. Let's do this!'

Liverpool cruised through the first few rounds but, in the quarter-finals, they faced Manchester United. United were the tournament favourites because they had won it so many times before. They didn't have many star attackers this time but they did have a strong defence with John Curtis and Ronnie Wallwork.

'Yes, but they haven't played against Mo yet!' Jamie reminded everyone in the dressing room. Michael Owen's reputation was growing but that didn't make it any easier to stop him.

If they could play it to Michael, he would score for sure. The Liverpool midfield just needed to win the ball and create enough chances for their star striker.

'No problem!' Jamie said confidently, looking at Thommo and the other Jamie.

Every time Manchester United tried to attack, Jamie was there to stop them with a tough tackle. He wasn't taking any prisoners. And once he had won the ball, Jamie looked for Michael's runs. With a great pass, he played Michael through. He was never going to miss. 1-0!

At the final whistle, Liverpool were through to the semi-finals, thanks to three goals from Michael.

'Nice one, hat-trick hero!' Jamie cheered as the players walked off the pitch.

'No, you guys did all the hard work,' Michael

replied modestly. 'I just finished things off!'

Liverpool weren't finished yet. After winning 7-5 on aggregate against Crystal Palace, they were through to the FA Youth Cup Final for only the third time in forty years.

'This time, we're going to lift that trophy!' Jamie told his teammates.

They just had to keep believing in themselves and beat West Ham. That wouldn't be easy because West Ham had young England stars Rio Ferdinand and Frank Lampard in their team. But the Liverpool players felt unstoppable.

'No team wants to play against us,' Steve told the players as they prepared for the biggest games of their careers. 'Those West Ham players are scared of us right now and they should be. We win every battle because we fight to the end!'

But in the build-up, the Liverpool youth coach had some difficult decisions to make. Michael couldn't play in the first leg and neither could their centre-back, Eddie Turkington.

'Do we have anyone else who could play in

defence?' Steve asked Hugh McAuley and Ronnie Moran.

'Jamie,' they both replied straight away.

'Really?'

'That lad could play anywhere!' Hugh exclaimed. 'He's already moved from striker to midfielder, so why not midfielder to defender? He reads the game so well and he's good in the air too. I think that might end up being his best position.'

Ronnie agreed and so it was settled; Jamie would play in defence for the Youth Cup Final. When he heard the news, Jamie was surprised but he didn't panic. He was very good at adapting and he would do whatever was best for his team. He worked hard in training to learn his new role, and listened to advice:

'You're too deep there, Jamie! You're playing them onside.'

'Don't get too tight to your marker. He'll spin and speed past you.'

'That's it! If Phil comes forward to win a header, you sweep round to cover his position.'

Soon, Jamie was enjoying his new position. From

central defence, he had a great view of the game and he could do even more tackling and shouting than before. However, playing that role in training was one thing. Playing that role in the FA Youth Cup Final was something completely different.

'Just stay calm, listen to Phil and use your football brain,' Steve advised him before kick-off at Upton Park. 'You're going to be great!'

Jamie was more excited than nervous as he ran out onto the pitch in front of 15,000 fans. This was his biggest challenge yet and there was no way that he was going to let his teammates down. They just had to stay organised in defence. As soon as the whistle went, Jamie started talking to the other centre-back, Liverpool's captain Phil Brazier.

'You mark Number Ten,' he told him, 'and I'll look out for the runners from midfield.'

Jamie and Phil didn't stop communicating until half-time. By then, Liverpool were 1-0 up.

'Your partnership is looking really solid at the back,' Steve told them. 'Just keep it up in the second half, lads!'

Jamie was on fire in his defensive debut. He won almost every header and every tackle for his team. He felt unbeatable, like he could win the ball off anyone. At the final whistle, Jamie celebrated his first clean sheet with Phil.

'Are you sure that was your first game in defence?' Phil joked. 'You look like you've been playing there for years!'

Even though 2-0 was a great result, the Youth Cup final wasn't over yet. They still had the second leg to play at Anfield and they wanted to win that too. This time, Michael was back up front and the team spirit was better than ever.

'Let's make sure that the trophy is ours!' Phil cried out and the other players cheered so loudly that the dressing room walls began to shake.

Jamie was pleased to be playing at centre-back again. He felt comfortable in his new role. As he ran out on to the pitch, Jamie turned and clapped the 20,000 Liverpool fans in the stadium. They were all here to watch their youth team win the cup and they were making plenty of noise.

But Liverpool got off to an awful start. West Ham had the ball on the edge of the penalty area. Jamie ran out bravely to make a block but Lampard's shot flew into the top corner. 2-1!

'Don't panic, boys!' Phil shouted at his teammates. 'We just need to stay disciplined.'

For the first time, Jamie felt nervous in his new role. A West Ham goal-kick bounced all the way into the Liverpool box. He mis-timed his jump and the striker shot just wide. Phil glared at his partner but he didn't need to say a word.

'Concentrate!' Jamie told himself.

After a few nice touches of the ball, his nerves quickly disappeared. Every time he intercepted a pass, he looked to start an attack. Liverpool got back into the game and Michael Owen and Mark Quinn made it 4-1 on aggregate. As Mark dived across the grass to celebrate, the whole team piled on top of him. It was definitely Liverpool's trophy now.

But Jamie didn't stop until the very end. Ferdinand ran forward down the right but Jamie came across to clear the danger. West Ham's left winger put the ball in the box but Jamie headed it away. When the referee blew the final whistle, Jamie ran to hug his teammates.

'We did it!' he cheered. It was the greatest feeling ever.

Jamie was at the back of the line as the players went up to collect their winner's medals. When the trophy was passed to him, he lifted it high into the air. Hopefully, it would be the first of many trophies at Liverpool.

Steve was delighted with Jamie's performances. 'I knew you'd be good but I didn't think you'd be *that* good. I think we've finally found your best position. You're a natural defender!'

CHAPTER 14

WELCOME TO THE FIRST TEAM!

'Roy Evans wants to see you,' Steve told Jamie one morning during the summer of 1996.

Roy Evans was the manager of the Liverpool first team. If he wanted to see you, it either meant really good news or really bad news. After their historic Youth Cup victory, Jamie felt sure that it must be good news.

'The gaffer asked to see me too!' Michael said excitedly.

'And me!' Thommo added.

'No way, they must have made a mistake, mate,' Jamie joked. 'You have to be over five feet tall to play in the Premier League!'

Thankfully, it *was* good news. When Jamie sat down in a chair in Roy's office, there was already a professional contract on the table with his name on it. He looked for the most important information: it was £750 a week! He tried to look cool but he was delighted with his pay rise.

'That's three times more than my current wage!' he thought to himself.

Ten minutes later, he walked out of the room with his brand-new deal. 'Come on, let's go and celebrate!' he told Thommo and Michael.

It was great to be Liverpool's top young prospects but they couldn't relax for long. They still had lots of hard work ahead of them. It was great to train with amazing first team players like Ian Rush, John Barnes, Robbie Fowler and Steve McManaman, but Jamie wanted more. He wanted to play alongside them for Liverpool in the Premier League.

'It's only a matter of time, son,' his dad Philly told him. 'Keep doing what you're doing and your chance will come.'

Because of his great attitude, Jamie quickly became

one of Ronnie Moran's favourites. Some youngsters thought the Liverpool first team coach was too strict and old-school but Jamie liked his style. If Ronnie said 'Run!', Jamie would run until he told him to stop. He gave 110 per cent effort at all times.

'What a tackle!' Ronnie shouted to him. 'That's it lads, you've got to be totally fearless!'

Jamie really respected the club's senior players but as soon as he stepped on to the training pitch, his shyness disappeared. He was so determined to show everyone that he was ready for his first team debut. Robbie and Macca were both local lads who had grown up to become Liverpool's biggest stars.

'I'm going to be next!' Jamie told his mum Paula. There was no doubt in his mind.

Every Friday morning, Ronnie took the food order for that weekend's pre-match meal. That's how the players found out if they were in the team or not. Every Friday morning, Jamie held his breath and crossed his fingers. Thommo was asked the question in August 1996. Finally, five months later, it was Jamie's turn.

'What do you want to eat tomorrow?'

He was so shocked at first that he forgot the answer that he had been practising for months. 'Ch-chicken and beans, please,' Jamie managed to say eventually.

Ronnie's face broke into a smile. 'Congratulations, lad – welcome to the first team!'

Jamie would happily have danced all the way home to tell his family the brilliant news. His name was on the teamsheet!

'My lad is going to make his Liverpool first team debut!' Philly cheered proudly. Soon, everyone in Bootle knew about it.

Jamie's nerves only began to shake during the long trip up to Middlesbrough. What if he made an awful error that lost them the match? No, he couldn't think like that. He had to be positive.

For seventy-five minutes, Jamie sat on the bench, waiting impatiently. Just as he began to think that he might not play, Ronnie called out to him: 'Get ready!'

Wearing the Number 23 shirt, Jamie ran on to replace Rob Jones at right-back. He would have played any position, maybe even goalkeeper. In the end, Liverpool lost 2-1 but Jamie was relieved and pleased about his own performance.

'Phew, I didn't make any bad mistakes,' he told his dad afterwards. 'I had nightmares about that!'

Three days later, Jamie was on the subs' bench again. This time, he came on at half-time and played in central midfield. Even though he still didn't have a fixed position, he was getting closer and closer to the starting line-up.

'I reckon you'll play the whole game up front next week!' his brother Paul joked.

Paul was nearly right. The day before Liverpool's match against Aston Villa, Roy had a chat with Jamie.

'It doesn't look like Bjørn Kvarme is going to be able to play, so I need you to replace him at centre-back,' the manager said. 'Are you up for the challenge?'

That was a silly question to ask Jamie. He was up for every challenge. 'Of course, boss!' he replied.

In the end, Bjørn was able to play after all but Jamie didn't move back to the bench – Patrik Berger was ill and so Jamie moved to midfield instead. Jamie's task was to keep Villa's star midfielder, Andy Townsend, quiet.

'He's one of the best players in the league!' Jamie thought to himself, panicking.

As he changed into his kit in the dressing room, his heart thudded loudly in his chest. He looked around, wondering if the other players could hear it. But they were all focused on their own pre-game routines.

As Jamie walked out of the tunnel, the Anfield roar sounded louder than ever. This was it – the big time. He needed to prove that he was good enough to wear the Liver Bird on his chest week in, week out.

As soon as the match kicked off, Jamie chased after his opponent. He launched into a crunching tackle and sent Townsend flying. The referee blew his whistle for a free kick and reached into his pocket. Jamie froze. Was he about to get the fastest ever red card? Fortunately, it was only a yellow.

'Calm down,' Jamie Redknapp, his midfield partner, warned him.

Jamie did as he was told and soon he was enjoying himself. Townsend made a few attacking runs but he wasn't dominating the game. At half-time, Roy patted Jamie on the back.

'More of the same in the second-half!' he demanded.

As Stig Inge Bjørnebye curled in a corner from the left, Jamie made a late run towards the front post. The Villa players didn't react until it was too late. When the ball arrived, Jamie headed it down into the bottom corner.

Goooooooooooooooooooaaaaaaaaaaaaaaaaaallllllllllll llllllllllllllll!!!!!!!!!!!!!!!!!!!!

He hadn't forgotten how to score! Jamie sprinted towards the corner flag with his arms up in the air. The fans at the Kop End were going wild for their new Anfield hero. He hadn't prepared for this moment. It seemed too good to be true. Macca was the first to hug him.

'Once a striker, always a striker!' he laughed.

Jamie smiled. Not only was he a Liverpool player, he was also now a Liverpool goalscorer.

CHAPTER 15

MR LIVERPOOL

'Well done, lad!' his dad shouted and clapped as Jamie walked into the Anfield players' lounge after the match. Philly had just seen his son score his first-ever goal for Liverpool. It didn't get much better than that. 'That's a moment I will never forget!'

'Thanks, Dad!' Jamie replied at a much quieter volume. He was just as excited, but he didn't want to embarrass himself in front of his new teammates.

After that dream start, Jamie didn't play again for the first team during the 1996–97 season. He wasn't too worried, though. He was still only nineteen and he was getting good experience in the reserves. He was already thinking ahead to the 1997–98 season.

'Our defence is getting old now,' he discussed with his dad during the summer break. 'Mark Wright is thirty-three and Razor Ruddock is nearly thirty.'

Philly agreed. 'You're right, they need fresh young lads like you!'

Jamie didn't play in every match of the 1997–98 season, but he did get a lot more game time. When Liverpool fell out of the title race, Roy turned to the future of the club: Jamie, Michael and Thommo. They were full of passion and energy and they never let their manager down.

Jamie wasn't even on the bench for the first Merseyside derby of the season but, by the time that Everton came to Anfield in February 1998, he was a regular.

'I really hope Roy picks me for the big game,' he told Thommo in training. 'I'm ready!'

Slowly, Jamie's love for Everton had faded. The glory days of Sharpy and Sheedy were over and he had fallen in love with Anfield instead. His coaches had made sure of that.

'Lad, you've got to start behaving like a Liverpool

player,' Hugh McAuley had told him when he was eighteen. It was time to get serious.

After that, Jamie had stopped asking about the Everton score on the team bus each Saturday. He was a red now, not a blue – and the Merseyside derby was his best chance to prove that.

Jamie was delighted when he saw his name on the teamsheet. He was starting at centre-back alongside Bjørn. Only a few minutes later, though, the panic set in.

'I've got to play against Duncan Ferguson!' Jamie realised.

'Big Dunc' was one of the toughest strikers in the Premier League. He was big, strong and often angry. It was definitely going to be Jamie's most difficult battle so far.

'Use your head, not your arms,' Mark Wright told him before the game. Wrighty was a calm, clever defender who had played over 150 games for Liverpool and he had lots of England caps too. Jamie was grateful for his good advice.

At half-time, it was 0-0. The plan was working and

Jamie was feeling comfortable at the back.

'You've done a great job so far!' Roy told him. 'Big Dunc has barely touched the ball.'

But after sixty minutes, Ferguson scored to make it 1-0 to Everton. Jamie threw himself bravely in front of the shot but he couldn't quite block it. As he lay on the grass, he hit the ground in frustration.

'That wasn't your fault,' Jamie Redknapp told him. 'Keep going, you're playing well.'

Jamie picked himself up and carried on. There was no way that he'd let 'Big Dunc' score again. Ten minutes later, Paul Ince scored an equaliser for Liverpool. A draw wasn't the result that Liverpool wanted but the manager was pleased with Jamie's performance.

'You showed lots of character today,' Roy told him. 'Well done!'

Roy's successor as Liverpool manager, Gérard Houllier, was an even bigger fan of Jamie's character. After only a month at Anfield, Gérard called him into his office.

'You're exactly what I want in my team,' he told

Jamie. 'I just wish I had more players with your aggression and spirit.'

Jamie was really pleased to have such support from his manager. They discussed Liverpool's strengths and weaknesses and Gérard promised him a new contract. Jamie couldn't wait for the new season to begin.

'He said that I'm one of Liverpool's first-choice centre-backs now!' he told his dad excitedly.

Jamie started the first league match and almost every other game after that. If he made a mistake, Gérard showed him the video and talked about what he could do better next time. With such detailed coaching, Jamie's defending improved rapidly. At the end of the 1998–99 season, Jamie was named Liverpool's Player of the Year. He hadn't expected to win such a big honour so early in his career.

'Thanks Gérard,' he said after proudly collecting his trophy. 'You've really helped me with my game.'

Jamie's centre-back days didn't last, however. As soon as Liverpool signed Sami Hyypiä and Stéphane Henchoz, he knew he was under pressure. He fought hard to keep his place but when Manchester United came to Anfield in September 1999, it all went wrong.

As Ryan Giggs crossed the ball from the left, Jamie knew that Andy Cole was behind him, waiting to score. Jamie tried to put it behind for a corner but the ball glanced off his head and flew into the bottom corner. Own goal!

As the United players celebrated, Jamie hung his head but there was nowhere to hide. It was his fault and all 35,000 Liverpool fans knew it. All he could do was try to put his mistake behind him and carry on. It wasn't easy but Jamie had plenty of spirit.

With seconds to go in the first half, Manchester United won a free-kick on the right. David Beckham curled a dangerous ball into the box and after a goalmouth scramble, it eventually bounced off Jamie and into the net. Another own goal!

Jamie was having an absolute nightmare at Anfield. He was tempted to just walk off the pitch and never come back. But that wasn't the Carragher way. Jamie thought back to that miserable day when he had faked an injury for Merton Villa. He had promised his dad that he would never be a coward again.

'It's just a bad day,' Jamie told himself. Every player had bad days. He just needed to stay focused and bounce back.

Gérard always believed in Jamie, but a few weeks later, he called Jamie in for another meeting.

'I'm going to play Sami and Stéphane against Chelsea,' the Liverpool manager revealed.

Jamie was very disappointed but he accepted the decision. 'Does that mean that I'm on the bench?' he asked.

Gérard shook his head, 'No, I want you to play at right-back.'

It was yet another new position for Jamie but he didn't complain. He would play anywhere to help his team.

CHAPTER 16

TROPHY TIME

Stevie Gerrard scored the first, Michael Owen got the second and Robbie Fowler grabbed the fourth. In December 2000, after beating champions Manchester United, Liverpool had now beaten Arsenal too.

'What a thrashing!' Jamie cheered happily. 'I'm the only local lad who didn't score today!'

Stevie was the latest star to move from the youth academy to the Liverpool first team. He was a central midfielder who loved a crunching tackle and a powerful shot.

'Basically, he's a much better version of me!' Jamie said modestly.

After a good spell at right-back, Jamie had moved again, this time to left-back. Gérard was desperate to have Jamie in the team somewhere. He was always up for a new challenge but this one was particularly tough.

'My left leg is just for balance,' he joked with Michael. 'It hasn't kicked a ball for years!'

Jamie was fine with the defensive part of his role; it was the attacking part that he found more difficult. He could pass the ball well but he wasn't very good at crossing. Every time he got forward, the ball either hit the first defender or flew over everyone's heads.

'Maybe just stick to the tackling next time!' Robbie laughed as Jamie kicked another ball straight off the training pitch.

Apart from his crossing, things were going very well for Liverpool. They hadn't won a major trophy for six years but, hopefully, that was about to change. The Arsenal victory put them third in the Premier League and they were still in three other competitions too: the League Cup, the FA Cup and the UEFA Cup.

'Fingers crossed, I'll win my first senior Liverpool trophy this season,' Jamie told Paul.

'You need to think bigger than that. At this rate, you could win four!' his brother replied.

In the League Cup Final in February 2001 they faced Championship side Birmingham City. Liverpool were the clear favourites to win and 40,000 of their fans travelled to Cardiff for the occasion. As he walked onto the pitch at the Millennium Stadium, Jamie could see so many red shirts in the crowd that he thought he was back at Anfield. Before kick-off, the supporters sang 'You'll Never Walk Alone'.

'This atmosphere is amazing!' Jamie thought to himself. Big finals were the best. He closed his eyes and clenched his fists. He was ready to win.

With two minutes to go in the game, Liverpool had a 1-0 lead thanks to Robbie. Jamie had put in a solid performance at left-back and he had one hand on his first senior trophy. But then Stéphane slid in for a bad tackle in the box. Penalty to Birmingham – 1-1! Jamie couldn't believe it but Liverpool had to keep going. Winning was all that mattered.

'Heads up, boys!' he shouted.

After extra time, the match went to penalties. Robbie agreed to take one, and so did Gary McAllister, Didi Hamann, Nicky Barmby and Christian Ziege.

'I want to take one,' Jamie said. He was desperate to help his team.

'Are you sure, mate?' Robbie asked him. His teammates trusted him completely in defence but he had only ever scored two goals for Liverpool in three years.

'I used to be a striker, remember,' Jamie argued. 'I had a great penalty record for Bootle Boys and you've seen what I can do in training!'

'Okay, you can take the sixth if it goes to sudden death,' the assistant manager Phil Thompson decided.

After ten penalties, the score was 4-4. It was Jamie's turn to take one. With his socks around his ankles, he made the long walk from the halfway line. He tried to look as calm as possible but inside, his heart was pounding. Jamie was still angry about

Liverpool's poor performance in the final. How had they failed to beat Birmingham in 120 minutes of football?

He placed the ball carefully on the spot and then walked back to the edge of the penalty area. It was a long run-up but that was Jamie's style. He sprinted towards the ball and hit his shot high into the top right corner. Goal! The Liverpool fans cheered but Jamie didn't even smile as he ran back to join his teammates.

'That was our best penalty yet!' Robbie cheered. 'I'm sorry that I ever doubted you. You've got nerves of steel.'

When Andy Johnson of Birmingham City missed his penalty, Liverpool were the League Cup winners. The whole team ran over to celebrate with the supporters. It was a special moment but Jamie felt more relieved than delighted. He was already thinking ahead to the next challenges.

'When we get to our next final, we'll have to play much better than that!' he told Stevie as Robbie lifted the cup.

Three months later, Liverpool were back in Cardiff to face Arsenal in the FA Cup Final.

'Dennis Bergkamp, Thierry Henry, Robert Pirès,' Jamie counted on his fingers, 'Freddie Ljungberg, Patrick Vieira. That's five superstars already! We're going to have to be at our absolute best to beat them.'

Fortunately, Liverpool's defence was looking very solid. Gérard picked the same four players in every game: Markus Babbel on the right, Sami and Stèphane in the middle and Jamie at left-back. By the time they faced Arsenal, they were united. That was the key to a successful backline.

'Up!' Sami shouted and the four of them moved forward together to play the strikers offside.

Ljungberg was Jamie's opponent in the final. The Swedish winger was quick and skilful but Jamie was clever and strong. It was a good battle and for the first seventy minutes, Jamie was winning. But suddenly, Ljungberg made a great run from deep to meet Pirès' pass. Jamie couldn't keep up as Ljungberg dribbled round the keeper. Jamie threw himself across the goal to block the shot but he couldn't stop it. 1-0 to Arsenal!

'We can't give the ball away like that!' Jamie shouted. They needed to focus and fight back in the last twenty minutes.

Usually, Jamie's first thought when he got the ball was to pass but Liverpool were running out of time. Instead, Jamie attacked down the left wing with a great burst of speed. Ray Parlour wasn't expecting that and fouled him. From the free-kick, Michael scored the equaliser. One-all! There was still time to get a winner but they had to be careful.

'Mark up!' Jamie shouted to his teammates, pointing to each opponent.

Arsenal had a free-kick and all of their attackers were up in the penalty area. But Liverpool were organised and quickly won the ball back. It was time for the counter-attack. Patrik Berger played an amazing through-ball for Michael and his shot curled into the bottom corner. Now it was 2-1!

'Mo, you're a hero!' Jamie screamed, lifting his friend into the air in front of the cheering fans.

But the match still wasn't over yet. 'Three more minutes, lads!' Jamie called out. It was time for the defenders to become the heroes. As Bergkamp dribbled into the penalty area, Jamie slid in to make a very important tackle. Ashley Cole crossed the ball back into the box but Jamie headed it away. There was no way that he was going to let Arsenal score again. The Liverpool fans chanted his name:

Carra! Carra! Carra!

Jamie was so tired that he could hardly run anymore but he didn't stop until the referee blew the final whistle.

'We've won the cup double!' he cried as the whole team joined together and jumped up and down. Victory felt amazing and made all the pain go away.

'And we can still win the treble!' the captain, Sami, reminded everyone.

The Liverpool players felt very confident ahead of the UEFA Cup Final against Alavés. When Markus and Stevie scored early goals to make it 2-0, Jamie hoped that it was game over. It was his fifty-seventh match of a very long season and his legs were desperate for a holiday.

'Let's keep it tight now, lads!' Jamie called out.

But the Liverpool defence was all over the place and that allowed Alavés to fight back. After ninety minutes, the score was 4-4. It was a very exciting game for the fans but Jamie didn't want extra-time. He just wanted it to be over.

'It's golden goal tonight,' Gérard told his tired players. 'So let's score before they do!'

The winner was an own goal but Liverpool didn't care. They had won their third trophy of the year.

'What a season!' Stevie said with a laugh. 'We don't make life easy for ourselves, though, do we?'

Jamie smiled. 'No, but we fight until the very end!'

It was that warrior spirit that had written their names into Liverpool's history books.

CHAPTER 1

COMING BACK
STRONGER

Jamie had been looking forward to playing in a World
Cup ever since he first started loving football. He had
watched Mexico 1986 and Italy 1990 on TV with
his dad and brothers. It looked magical and the 2002
tournament seemed a realistic target.

'I'll be twenty-four by then and we'll lead England
to victory!' Jamie had said to Michael during their
youth days at Liverpool.

Now, that dream looked like it might come true.
Jamie had captained the England Under-21s for years
and he now had six senior caps too. After winning
the treble with Liverpool, he had become a regular
in the national squad. The England manager Sven-

Göran Eriksson liked Jamie's spirit and his versatility.

'It's great to have someone who can play anywhere across the defence,' Sven told him.

Jamie was very proud to be playing for his country. England had a brilliant first-choice back four – Gary Neville, Rio Ferdinand, Sol Campbell and Ashley Cole – but he was ready to step up if there were any injuries or suspensions.

'You can always rely on me!' Jamie promised his manager.

However, as the World Cup approached, Jamie had an injury of his own. His knee had been troubling him for a while but he had played on through the pain.

'We've got a good chance of winning the league!' Jamie argued with Gérard. 'There's no way I'm resting until I absolutely have to.'

But by the end of the 2001–2 Premier League season, the problem was getting worse.

'You're going to need an operation,' the Liverpool physio warned him.

Jamie wasn't surprised. After each match he

played, he could hardly walk the next day. 'Okay, but can it wait until after the World Cup?' he asked.

'You'll have to speak to Gérard about that. If you wait until August, you'll miss at least the first month of next season.'

Jamie felt really torn between club and country. He was desperate to play at a major international tournament but he didn't want to let Liverpool down. He was also worried about losing his place in the starting line-up. After lots of discussions, Jamie made up his mind. He would have the operation in June instead of going to South Korea and Japan.

'We can watch the tournament together on TV,' Stevie said, trying to cheer him up. He was having an operation too. 'We'll be back for the 2006 World Cup!'

Jamie was pleased to have his Liverpool teammate around. But as they supported England from the sofa, they couldn't help thinking 'What if'.

'With Gary injured, I could have been the first-choice right-back!' Jamie said as they watched Danny Mills playing there instead.

'And I could have been playing in central midfield with Scholesy!' Stevie said as they watched Nicky Butt playing there instead.

When England lost to Brazil in the World Cup quarter-finals, Jamie turned his attention back to Liverpool. Once the doctors were happy with the operation, he began his recovery. He spent long, boring days in the gym at Melwood, dreaming about winning more trophies.

'It will all be worth it if I make it back for the start of the season,' he told his family.

In the end, however, he missed the first month of the new season and it wasn't easy to win his place back in the team. John Arne Riise was playing well at left-back, scoring goals and setting them up with his dangerous crosses. The Norwegian was a great attacking option but Jamie wasn't giving up that easily.

'Well, it's a good thing I can play anywhere!' he said to Michael.

He would do anything to play in the team. In the 2003 League Cup Final against Manchester United,

Jamie was selected at right-back. His job was to mark Ryan Giggs out of the game.

'A nice easy task then!' he joked, thinking about the winger's wondergoal against Arsenal back in 1999.

But back at the Millennium Stadium in Cardiff, Jamie had another brilliant game. He won every header and used his strength and experience to keep Giggs quiet. At the other end, Stevie and Michael got the goals to seal the win.

'What a team performance!' Gérard said with a big smile on his face. Liverpool had outplayed the Premier League champions.

As Sami lifted the cup, Jamie stood just behind him, jumping up and down like crazy. It was definitely their best final victory. After his injury problems and the disappointment of missing the World Cup, he couldn't wait to hold the trophy.

'Liverpool! Liverpool!' he cheered again and again when it was finally in his hands.

At the start of the 2003–4 season, Jamie was on the move again. New signing Steve Finnan was a right-back, so Jamie moved back to the left. It was frustrating to keep changing positions but he tried to stay positive.

'As long as I'm playing, I don't mind where!' was his attitude once again.

In September 2003, Liverpool were drawing 1-1 with Blackburn when the ball came to Jamie in defence. As he went to clear it downfield, Lucas Neill flew in with a horror tackle on his right leg.

'Arghhhhhhhhhhhhhhhhhhhhhhhhhh!' Jamie cried out. He was in absolute agony.

He wasn't the kind of player that faked an injury, so his teammates knew it must be serious. Neill got a red card but that didn't help Jamie.

'I really need that magic spray!' he groaned.

With the help of two Liverpool coaches, he hobbled over to the touchline. Unfortunately, the Liverpool physio was already dealing with another injury.

'I can go back on,' Jamie told Gérard.

'Are you sure? We've got John Arne on the bench–'

'Yes, I'm fine!'

But Jamie wasn't fine. Five minutes later, he had to be substituted. On the treatment table, the news wasn't good.

'I'm afraid the leg is broken,' the physio told him.

Jamie stared down at the floor. 'How long will I be out for?' he asked eventually. He wasn't sure that he wanted to hear the answer. Life without football felt unbearable.

'Let's not worry about that yet...'

'Weeks? Months?'

The physio frowned. 'It's going to be months, I'm afraid.'

At first, Jamie was devastated. He hated the idea of Liverpool playing and winning without him. But eventually, he accepted his situation. He had to stay positive and focus on the future.

'I'll just have to come back even stronger!' he said.

CHAPTER 18

RAFA'S REVOLUTION

'Thanks for coming,' Rafa Benitez said. Euro 2004 was about to start but the new Liverpool manager had travelled to Portugal for a meeting with the club's three senior players – Stevie, Michael and Jamie.

After listening carefully to their opinions about the team, Rafa made his speech. 'I truly believe that I can turn things around at Liverpool. That's why I took the job. With a few changes, we can win major trophies but I really need your support.'

Jamie was impressed. He had previously played against Rafa's brilliant Valencia team and the new Liverpool manager's plans seemed exciting and ambitious.

Stevie and Michael, however, weren't so sure. They believed that Liverpool needed more than a few changes to challenge the best teams in Europe. Meanwhile, Chelsea were desperate to sign Stevie and after six seasons at Anfield, he was close to leaving.

'I want to win the Premier League and the Champions League,' Stevie admitted. 'I'm just not sure I can do that at Liverpool.'

'We can,' Rafa assured him.

Michael, too, was seeking new challenges. He was a transfer target for Real Madrid and, although he loved Anfield, he was tempted by the chance to join *Los Galácticos.*

Before all of that, though, the Liverpool lads had Euro 2004 to win. Michael and Stevie played every game for England but, in contrast, Jamie didn't play a single minute.

'I didn't come here for a boring holiday,' he moaned to Stevie.

It was frustrating for Jamie to leave his friends and family behind just to sit on the bench for two weeks.

He wanted to play and he believed that he was good enough to play. With Rio unavailable, why wasn't he partnering Sol at the back? Jamie was disappointed when England lost to Portugal in the quarter-finals but at least he got to go home to Liverpool.

'It's time to see how Rafa's revolution is going,' he told Michael.

When they returned to training at Melwood, there were lots of exciting new faces in the Liverpool team. Strikers Djibril Cissé and Fernando Morientes would hopefully bring more goals to the team, while Xabi Alonso and Luis García were skilful Spanish midfielders.

'What do you think?' Stevie asked Jamie after their first session. 'Xabi looks really good!'

Jamie was only thinking about his competition in defence. 'I'm not sure about Josemi and Mauricio Pellegrino is thirty-four. I'm not too worried!'

When Stevie agreed to stay at Liverpool, Jamie was very relieved. They were good friends and losing their superstar skipper would have been an absolute disaster. However, there was still bad news to come.

'I've thought long and hard about it and I still want to sign for Real,' Michael told Jamie just before the start of the new season.

'Are you sure, Mo?' Jamie asked. He really didn't want his best mate to leave. 'They've already got Raúl and Ronaldo up front. You might not play as many games as you would here.'

Michael shrugged. 'Sorry mate, I just need a new challenge.'

Jamie understood. He never thought about leaving Liverpool but he knew that it would be hard to say no to a club like Real Madrid. Jamie wished Michael well and focused on the season ahead.

'Boss, where will I be playing?' he asked. Most players already knew their position but Jamie always had to check.

At first, Rafa wanted him at right-back but before their first Premier League match against Tottenham, he changed his mind. 'You'll be playing at centre-back with Sami,' the manager told him.

Jamie was delighted. Ever since the Youth Cup Final, he had always preferred playing in the middle of the defence and now he was back where he belonged. He couldn't wait to prove it and stay there for years to come.

Rafa believed in Jamie but he highlighted key areas for improvement.

'I want you to watch these carefully,' the Liverpool manager told him, handing over a pile of AC Milan DVDs from the 1980s. 'See how Franco Baresi reads the game and organises the players around him.'

Jamie always liked learning more about football. It was like being a kid again and reading *Shoot!* magazine every week. As the season went on, he could feel himself getting better and better. Jamie was still as aggressive and hard-working as ever, but he was also more intelligent with his sense of movement.

'If I didn't know you better, I'd call you classy!' Sami joked. They were enjoying the chance to reform their solid partnership.

As vice-captain, Jamie was more of a leader than ever. Many of their new signings weren't used to the fast and physical style of English football. It was

Jamie's job to teach them 'The Liverpool Way' and he was very happy to help:

'Don't mess around with it back there!'

'You've got to be stronger there – he's pushed you off the ball!'

'Don't stop, keep chasing!'

In the Premier League, Liverpool were far too inconsistent. They beat top teams like Arsenal and Everton but lost to Birmingham City, Middlesbrough and Crystal Palace. It didn't help that Rafa kept rotating his players.

'I don't need to rest,' Stevie complained, 'and I definitely don't *want* to!'

Jamie laughed. 'Tell me about it! But at least we've still got the Champions League!'

That was their shining light at the end of a difficult first season under Rafa.

CHAPTER 19

CHAMPIONS OF EUROPE

'Why can't we play like this in the Premier League too?' Jamie asked Stevie in February 2005 as they celebrated another Champions League victory against Bayer Leverkusen.

Stevie shrugged. He didn't understand it either but he was really enjoying Liverpool's European adventure. 'Let's just keep winning and work that out later!'

That wasn't easy, however, because their opponents were getting better and better. In the quarter-finals, they faced Italian giants Juventus. Jamie did his homework and looked forward to the challenge.

'Alessandro Del Piero, Pavel Nedved and Zlatan Ibrahimović,' he discussed with Sami ahead of the first leg at Anfield. 'We're playing against the big boys now!'

'Yes, but we can beat anyone!' his centre-back partner replied.

It was true. Together, they stopped Juventus's superstar strikers and Sami even got forward to score a goal.

'What a strike!' Jamie screamed as he chased after his teammate.

Liverpool won 2-1 in that first leg but they had a difficult trip to Italy ahead of them. Jamie and Sami would have to be at their very best again, especially as Stevie was out injured.

'We've got nothing to fear tonight!' Sami told the players in the dressing room before kick-off. They could hear the loud, aggressive chanting of the Juventus fans through the walls. It was easy to see why away teams often struggled at the Stadio Delle Alpi.

'If we stay organised, we can win this,' Jamie said to Sami. That's what they did best. It was all about teamwork.

Jamie headed away every cross that came in from

the right and Sami headed away every cross from the left. If an attacker got past Jamie, Sami was there to cover. If an attacker got past Sami, Jamie was there to cover.

'Lads, you're playing a blinder!' Xabi told them at half-time. Their great defensive work was inspiring the whole team.

Jamie carried on his man-of-the-match display in the second half. As Nedv d dribbled into the penalty area, he stopped him with a perfectly timed tackle. As the ball fell to Del Piero in the box, he jumped in bravely to block the shot. When the final whistle went, the score was still 0-0. Against the odds, Liverpool had made it through to the Champions League semi-finals.

Sami ran over and gave Jamie a massive hug.

'We did it!' he cheered.

The Liverpool fans stayed behind in the stadium to clap the players and sing song after song. Jamie used the last of his energy to smile and nod. It felt amazing to be a Liverpool hero.

Stevie was back for the semi-finals against Chelsea,

the club that he almost signed for. Their manager, José Mourinho, told the media that they would beat Liverpool easily.

'We'll see about that, won't we lads?' Jamie laughed. Chelsea's arrogance was only making them more determined to win.

At Stamford Bridge, Jamie and Sami were as solid as ever. Didier Drogba was strong and quick but they handled him well.

At the end of the first half, Jamie went up for a free-kick. As Stevie crossed the ball into the box, Ricardo Carvalho wrestled Jamie to the floor.

'Penalty!' Jamie screamed but the referee said no.

He was furious as he sprinted back to defence. 'That was definitely a foul!' he complained to Sami.

But Jamie had to stay focused because there was lots more work to do. When Drogba flicked the ball on, it looked like Mateja Kežman was going to score, but Jamie sprinted across to the rescue.

'Yes, Carra!' Stevie cheered.

The match finished 0-0. Liverpool had the result that they wanted.

'Great work, lads,' Rafa told them. 'Now we just have to win at Anfield!'

When Luis scored after four minutes, the Liverpool fans went wild. Jamie was delighted too but he knew what was coming next – eighty-six minutes of tough defending.

'Come on lads, no mistakes!' he shouted.

With the roaring crowd behind them, every Liverpool player gave 110 per cent. Chelsea attacked again and again but they couldn't get past Jamie and Sami. It was the longest ninety minutes of Jamie's life but the feeling at the end was unbelievable.

'We're in the Champions League final!' he screamed as the Liverpool players danced around the pitch together. It had been another amazing team effort.

The party went on for hours but eventually, it was time to think about the final. As Jamie looked through the AC Milan squad, he couldn't help feeling worried.

'They've got incredible players in every position!' he told Stevie.

'Every side we've played against looks better than us on paper,' his captain reminded him. 'But we've beaten them all because of our team spirit and because of our fans. Believe!'

Stevie was right. There was no point worrying about Kaká and Andriy Shevchenko. If Liverpool played their best football, they could win against anyone. They just had to stay calm and positive.

In the dressing room in Istanbul, Jamie looked around. Stevie, Sami and Xabi looked pumped up for the biggest game of their lives but a few of the younger players looked nervous.

'You okay, mate?' Jamie asked their left-back, Djimi Traoré.

Djimi just nodded. 'You're going to be fine,' Jamie told him.

But in the very first minute, Djimi gave away a free-kick and Paolo Maldini scored.
1-0! Jamie was shocked but he knew what his team needed from him.

'Come on, heads up, lads!' he shouted.

Unfortunately, things soon got worse. For the first time all season in the Champions League, the Liverpool defence wasn't playing as an organised unit. AC Milan took full advantage. When Hernán Crespo scored, Jamie was trying to mark two men at once.

'You can't leave me outnumbered like that!' he screamed at his teammates.

Five minutes later, Crespo scored again. Jamie stretched out his leg to try to intercept Kaká's brilliant through-ball but he couldn't quite reach it. 3-0! Jamie covered his face with his hands. It was turning into the worst day of his life.

At half-time, the AC Milan fans partied like the final was already over. The Liverpool players walked to the dressing room in silence.

Rafa's team talk was simple: 'Keep your heads up and remember that you play for Liverpool. Believe in yourselves and do it for the thousands of fans out there.'

The players sat and listened to the noise of their supporters. They sang 'You'll Never Walk Alone' over and over again. They hadn't given up yet. Jamie and the others were ready to fight back in the second half.

Stevie made it 3-1 with a brilliant header. As he ran back for the restart, he urged the fans to make more noise. Liverpool's passion and spirit was back. Two minutes later, Vladimír Šmicer made it 3-2.

'It's not over yet!' Jamie kept telling his teammates.

When he won the ball, he didn't just clear it down the field. Rafa had taught him how to be a better footballer than that. Instead, he played a neat pass and kept running forward for the one-two. Liverpool had nothing to lose now.

Milan Baroš was in the penalty area, calling for the ball. As he dribbled up the pitch, Jamie played the perfect pass. Milan flicked it to Stevie, who was fouled. Penalty! Xabi's spot-kick was saved but he scored the rebound. Three-all! It was the greatest comeback ever but they still needed one more goal to win.

'We can do this!' Jamie shouted.

By extra time, the Liverpool players were exhausted. AC Milan attacked again and again but Jamie stayed strong. Shevchenko passed to Crespo, who dribbled forward. It was three against two –

surely they would score. Jamie would have to be very clever to prevent the goal.

The angle was too tight for Crespo to shoot, so Jamie predicted that he would cut it back to Kaká. He was correct. As the ball came towards Kaká, Jamie stretched out his leg to make a crucial interception.

'What a tackle, Carra!' Stevie yelled. 'Keep going!'

Later on, Jamie made another brilliant sliding block.

'Arghhhhhhhhhhhhhhhhhh!' he cried out. He had cramp in his leg.

A minute later, Jamie had to stretch the same leg again to deny Shevchenko. He was in so much pain that he could barely run, but he refused to let his teammates down. Thanks to Jamie's heroics, Liverpool held on for penalties.

'I want to take one,' Jamie said straight away but the manager said no.

'You've done an amazing job tonight,' Rafa told him. 'Now, it's up to our attackers.'

Jamie stood with his teammates on the halfway

line as AC Milan missed and Liverpool scored. He punched the air.

'This is our night!' he told himself.

When Jerzy Dudek saved Shevchenko's penalty, Jamie was the first player to run and hug the Liverpool keeper. He wasn't tired anymore; he was buzzing.

'We're the Champions of Europe!' Jamie cheered. It was hard to believe but it was true. It didn't get any better than that.

He hurdled the advertising boards to celebrate with the Liverpool fans. After all, they had played such an important part in the victory. Somehow, amongst the thousands of joyful faces, Jamie spotted his brother Paul and his cousin Jamie. He was so pleased that they were sharing this special moment with him.

Carra! Carra! Carra!

As they did their lap of honour, Jamie and Stevie lifted the trophy together. They held one handle each and kissed the trophy at the same time. Liverpool's local lads had achieved the impossible and they didn't ever want to let go.

CHAPTER 20

JAMIE AND STEVIE

We all Dream of a Team of Carraghers,
A Team of Carraghers,
A Team of Carraghers!

After that unbelievable night in Istanbul in May 2005, Jamie had become a true Liverpool legend. The fans rewarded him with a song of his own.

'I've made it now!' he told Stevie as they listened for the first time.

Defenders hardly ever got to be the superstars, so Jamie enjoyed every minute of it. He even saw young fans wearing '23 CARRAGHER' on their backs. It was so nice to feel appreciated for all his hard work at the back. Goalscorers weren't the only heroes.

'Just don't get too comfortable,' Stevie joked. 'One more own goal and they won't be singing anymore!'

Michael had been Jamie's best friend at Liverpool for years until he left for Real Madrid. Since then, Stevie had taken his place. He was two years younger than Jamie but they were similar characters. With their passion, talent and determination, they were the perfect symbols of Liverpool Football Club.

'Trust me, you don't want to go to Chelsea,' Jamie told Stevie. The transfer rumours were back. 'We beat them in the semis, remember. *We* are the Champions of Europe, not them!'

Ahead of the 2005–6 season, captain and vice-captain signed new four-year contracts together. That was enough to fill the Liverpool fans with confidence.

'We're going to win the Premier League this season!' they predicted.

In defence, the Reds were better than ever. From October to December, Jamie and co. kept eight Premier League clean sheets in a row. Liverpool beat Everton in the Merseyside Derby but Jamie was still furious:

'How did we let them score?' he moaned to Sami.

Jamie enjoyed keeping clean sheets in the same way that strikers enjoyed scoring goals. It was a satisfying achievement that showed he had done his job well.

With Jamie starring in defence and Stevie starring in midfield, all that was missing was a super striker. But sadly, when Michael returned to England from Real, he decided to join Newcastle United instead.

At the end of the season, Liverpool finished third in the league but they reached the FA Cup Final. Jamie couldn't wait to return to Cardiff's Millennium Stadium.

'We always win at that stadium!' he reminded his teammates.

The Liverpool players were in for a shock, though, as their opponents West Ham started the game brilliantly. As Lionel Scaloni crossed from the right, Jamie knew that he had to intercept it. Marlon Harewood was waiting behind him for a tap-in. Jamie tried to kick the ball with his right foot but he missed it. Instead, the ball bounced off his left foot and trickled into the net. 1-0 to West Ham!

Jamie lay on the grass and hung his head. How

could he carry on after such a terrible mistake?

'Keep your head up!' Stevie said, putting an arm around his shoulder. 'Don't worry, we've got plenty of time to turn this around.'

Liverpool were losing 2-0 when Stevie's next comeback began. First he played an amazing pass to set up Djibril Cissé. Then, in the second half, he scored himself from the edge of the penalty area.

'Game on!' Stevie shouted as he ran back for kick-off.

Liverpool went in search of a winner but out of nowhere, West Ham took the lead again. In injury time, Jamie was on the verge of losing at the Millennium Stadium. However, with their Captain Fantastic still on the pitch, he wasn't giving up yet.

'Get it to Stevie!' Jamie yelled.

When the ball came to him, Stevie was over thirty yards from goal. Jamie had seen his friend score so many goals from that distance in training. Could Stevie do it again? He watched as the ball flew low and hard into the bottom corner. Three-all!

'You beauty!' Jamie screamed, jumping up onto Stevie's back.

After that the FA Cup Final was essentially over.
West Ham missed three penalties in the shoot-out
and the trophy was theirs. Jamie was so relieved that
he jumped into the air. Lots of Liverpool players ran
to thank their keeper Pepe Reina but he ran straight
to Stevie instead.

'Thanks mate, you really saved me today!' Jamie said.

Stevie winked. 'No problem, that's what
teammates are for! You've saved me loads of times
over the years.'

'That was something special, though. I think you
were even better than in Istanbul. They'll call that
"The Gerrard Final"!'

After lifting the trophy, the real party started down
on the pitch.

'Carra, grab one handle,' Stevie screamed over the
sound of the singing. 'Let's go!'

Just like they had in Istanbul a year earlier,
Liverpool's favourite local lads did a lap of honour,
raising and kissing the trophy together. Jamie and
Stevie – two Liverpool legends.

CHAPTER 21

ENGLAND

'I hope I play in at least one match this time!' Jamie said to Stevie as they travelled to Germany for the 2006 World Cup.

Jamie hadn't forgotten about his Euro 2004 disappointment. He loved representing his country but it wasn't much fun being one of England's back-up defenders. His chances of playing at centre-back didn't look good. Rio and John Terry would be the starters, with Sol and Jamie on the bench.

'Yes, but you can play right or left-back too,' Stevie reminded him.

Sometimes, Jamie hated being so versatile, but

he didn't feel that way when Gary Neville injured
his calf in training. It was the day before England's
second match against Trinidad and Tobago.

'This is your chance,' the manager Sven-Göran
Eriksson told Jamie, handing him the right-back role.

After seven years in the England squad, Jamie
was finally ready for his biggest moment. He walked
out on to the pitch in Nuremberg with Number 15
on his back and the three lions on his chest. He
sang the national anthem loud and proud, with his
arms around his teammates' shoulders. Playing in
a World Cup match with his best mates Stevie and
Michael; life didn't get much better than that.

'Come on, let's win this!' Jamie shouted.

He was as solid as ever in defence but after a long
Premier League season, Jamie didn't have the energy
to run up and down the right. After sixty minutes,
the score was still 0-0 and Sven decided to make an
attacking substitution. Winger Aaron Lennon came
on to replace Jamie.

'Well played,' Sven-Göran Eriksson told him as he
walked off.

Jamie was pleased with the praise but he hated coming off, even when he was so hot and tired. He watched from the bench as Peter Crouch and Stevie gave England a 2-0 win.

'You did a great job out there, lad,' his dad Philly said after the match. The whole Carragher family had travelled to Germany for the tournament. They were having a great time on holiday. 'They shouldn't have taken you off!'

Jamie played the full ninety minutes in England's 2-2 draw with Sweden. In the last fifteen minutes, he was exhausted but they had already made all their substitutions.

'Keep going!' Stevie told him.

Jamie nodded and struggled on until the end. Letting his teammates down was never an option.

With Gary Neville still injured, Jamie was expecting to start at right-back in England's Round of 16 match against Ecuador but Sven picked midfielder Owen Hargreaves instead.

'He's not even a defender!' Jamie complained to Michael. 'What did I do wrong?'

Being dropped from the team was so disappointing but Jamie didn't just give up. He came on for the last fifteen minutes to help the team hold on for a 1-0 win.

'We did it!' Stevie cheered at the final whistle. 'We're in the quarter-finals!'

Jamie wasn't surprised to be back on the bench against Portugal. But when John Terry started limping early in the match, Jamie became excited. Was he finally going to get his chance in his favourite position, centre-back? But Sven turned and told Sol to get ready instead.

'I don't know why I get my hopes up,' Jamie grumbled to himself. 'They'll never pick me!'

Just when he had accepted that he wouldn't get to play, Sven told Jamie to get ready. He was surprised because there was only one minute left in extra time.

'You'll be taking one of our penalties, okay?' the manager warned him.

Jamie nodded. If someone asked him to do something for his team, he never said no. Besides, he scored every time in training.

By the time Jamie walked to the spot, England had already missed two penalties. They couldn't miss another.

Jamie focused on his normal routine. Just as he had in the League Cup Final against Birmingham City, he walked to the edge of the penalty area, turned and started his long run-up. He struck the ball powerfully into the corner of the net but the goalkeeper hadn't even moved.

'You have to wait until I blow my whistle,' the referee told him. 'Take it again.'

Jamie groaned. What should he do now? Shoot into the same corner again or go for the other side? At the last second, Jamie decided to go with the second option but it didn't go well. He tried to place his shot instead of smashing the ball like normal. That was a big mistake. It was too close to the Portugal keeper, who made a good save.

Jamie put his hands to his face. What a nightmare!

'Never mind, mate,' Stevie said as Jamie slowly joined his teammates on the halfway line again. He had missed his penalty too.

Cristiano Ronaldo scored and England were out of the World Cup.

As the team travelled home, Jamie thought about his England career so far. He was proud to represent the nation but he found it very frustrating. How long did he want to keep going if he couldn't play at centre-back? That was his position now, not full-back or defensive midfield. Plus, he was twenty-eight years old and he wanted to make sure that his Liverpool career lasted many more years.

Jamie decided to give England's new manager, Steve McClaren, a chance before making his final decision. He was playing really well for Liverpool and if John or Rio got injured or suspended, hopefully Jamie would be moved up to the starting line-up. Then if he played well, he might stay there. He believed that he deserved that chance.

Unfortunately, however, it didn't work out like that. Steve kept Jamie at right-back and when there was an injury in the centre, he played Ledley King instead. Jamie had had enough.

'I'm sorry but I won't be available for England anymore,' he told Steve.

The England manager was shocked. 'Wait, don't decide yet!' he pleaded. 'You'll play ninety minutes at centre-back against Germany, I promise. You're my third-choice centre-back.'

Jamie was happy to hear that but, even so, Steve was too late. Jamie had made up his mind. After thirty-four England caps, his international career was over.

CHAPTER 22

ANOTHER EUROPEAN ADVENTURE

It was March 2007. Anfield was full to the brim, a red-hot cauldron of noise. Spanish giants Barcelona were in town and Liverpool once again had the chance to make it through to the Champions League quarter-finals. After winning the first leg they now had to stop Barca's superstar attackers a second time: Ronaldinho, Samuel Eto'o and youngster Lionel Messi.

'No problem!' Jamie said to Stevie confidently. 'We've done it before and we can do it again.'

He was thinking back to their European glory in 2005, when Liverpool had beaten the best teams in Europe because of their solid defence and organisation.

Sadly, this time Jamie would have to do it without Sami by his side. He had a new partner now, Danish defender Daniel Agger. They worked well together. Daniel brought pace and strength, while Jamie brought passion and experience.

'We can't switch off for a single second against these guys,' he told Daniel before kick-off. 'If we do, they'll destroy us.'

Stevie was Liverpool's captain but Jamie was their defensive leader. He made sure that everyone was tracking back and picking up their markers. By half-time, his throat was sore from all the shouting. But the '0-0' on the scoreboard showed that it had been worth it.

'Another half like that and we'll win this,' Rafa told his players. 'Just keep going. Jamie, you're having one of your big European nights!'

His manager was right; he was playing another blinder. Jamie was winning every tackle and every header against the best strikers in the world. Liverpool deserved to win but after seventy-five minutes, Barcelona took the lead.

'Stay calm,' Jamie told his fellow defenders. 'If it stays like this, we win on away goals. Just keep it tight!'

As the Liverpool fans grew more and more anxious, they cheered each tackle and block. And they cheered the name of their hero, their star defender:

Carra! Carra! Carra!

At the final whistle, the players hugged and the Anfield crowd roared. Liverpool had lost the match but they were through to the next round of the Champions League.

'What did I tell you?' Jamie joked with Stevie as they walked around the pitch, thanking the supporters. 'We can do it again!'

Soon, they were through to the semi-finals against... Chelsea.

'Not again!' Stevie moaned. Their English rivals would be desperate for revenge but Jamie was looking forward to the two matches.

'Just imagine how good the atmosphere will be for the Anfield leg!' he said excitedly.

At Stamford Bridge, Liverpool were under attack from the very beginning. As Drogba dribbled towards their goal, Jamie backed away. When he was younger, he might have dived in for a silly tackle but he was much more patient and sensible now. Working with Sami and Rafa had taught Jamie to wait for the right moment to steal the ball.

Just before Drogba entered the penalty area, he moved the ball from his right foot to his left.

'He'll need it back on his right foot to shoot,' Jamie predicted quickly. He always did his homework on strikers before he played against them.

He was correct. As Drogba moved the ball back to his right foot, Jamie made the important interception. The Chelsea striker cried out for a penalty but the referee said no. Jamie had used his experience to win the ball cleanly.

'Great work, Carra!' Daniel shouted.

In the end, Chelsea did score but there was nothing Jamie could do to stop it. He kept playing well and made sure that his team didn't concede a second. Liverpool were satisfied with the result.

'Now we just have to win at home!' Rafa encouraged his players.

When Daniel scored in the first half of the second leg, the Anfield crowd went wild. Liverpool only needed one more goal to make it through to the Champions League final again.

'What a strike!' Jamie congratulated his partner in defence. 'If we keep Drogba and Kalou quiet, hopefully our attackers can grab another.'

Stevie, Xabi and Dirk Kuyt did their best but even after extra time, the score was still 1-1 on aggregate. Liverpool would have to win yet another penalty shoot-out.

'I'll take one,' Jamie reminded Rafa, but his manager already knew that he was willing.

In the end, Jamie wasn't needed. Liverpool scored their first four spot-kicks and Chelsea only scored one.

'Two European finals in three years!' Jamie cheered as the whole team celebrated with the fans. 'Are you glad that you stayed, Stevie?'

His friend smiled. 'I'll answer that once we've won the final!'

Liverpool's opponents would be AC Milan, the

same team that they had beaten in the final two years earlier.

'First Chelsea again in the semi-finals and now Milan again in the final,' Jamie said. 'How spooky is that!'

'Never mind that,' Stevie argued. 'Think how determined they are going to be to beat us this time!'

It was true. Liverpool had fought back to steal the trophy in 2005 and now AC Milan wanted revenge. 'Yes, but we're determined to beat them *too*!' Jamie replied.

He couldn't wait to fight another huge European battle. Milan's new striker Pippo Inzaghi wasn't as skilful or quick as Shevchenko and Crespo, but he was very clever. If he got a chance in the six-yard box, he would definitely score.

'Do you remember our performances against Barcelona and Chelsea?' Jamie asked Daniel. 'We have to be that good again tonight, if not even better!'

It was looking good for Liverpool as half-time approached. But then Inzaghi deflected Andrea Pirlo's free-kick into the net.

'I can't believe it,' Jamie said as the players walked off the pitch. 'That was the flukiest goal ever!'

'We've just got to keep going,' Stevie told them in the dressing room. 'We don't deserve to be losing and we've got forty-five minutes to turn things around. Let's do this!'

Stevie and Dirk had good chances to equalise for Liverpool but as time ran out, so did their energy. On that hot evening in Athens, the players were exhausted. As Kaká played a brilliant through-ball to Inzaghi, Jamie tried to play the striker off-side but he timed his run perfectly and scored. Jamie kicked the air in frustration. It was 2-0 to AC Milan and probably game over.

Liverpool pulled one goal back but it was too little, too late. Jamie was very disappointed to lose in the final but this time, they just hadn't played well enough to win. Afterwards, he walked around the pitch with his teammates, clapping the fans. Despite the defeat, they carried on singing. As always, Jamie had done his best and that was all the Liverpool supporters ever asked of their players.

CHAPTER 23

BATTLING UNTIL THE END

'Congratulations, mate!' Stevie said, handing Jamie the Liverpool captain's armband for the day.

It was a very proud moment for Jamie and his family. After nearly twenty years at Anfield, he was making his 500th Liverpool appearance.

'I guess this makes me a veteran now!' he joked with Stevie.

Jamie was about to turn thirty but he still felt like he had many more years of top-level football ahead of him. He was playing more matches than ever and his passion for the game was still just as strong. As part of the Liverpool team, Jamie had won the Champions League, the FA Cup and the League Cup but there was one major trophy missing – the Premier League title. That was his ultimate dream.

'Every season, we get close but then something goes wrong,' Jamie discussed with his dad. 'We get injuries and we start losing games. Our defence isn't the problem; it's our attack.'

'Torres should help with that!' Philly replied.

Spanish striker Fernando Torres was their £20million signing from Atlético Madrid. He was the goalscorer that Liverpool had been missing ever since Michael Owen had left to join Real Madrid.

'That guy is world-class!' Stevie declared excitedly after a few training sessions with Fernando.

A great new Liverpool line-up was taking shape. With Xabi and Javier Mascherano playing together in front of Jamie's defence, Rafa moved Stevie forward into attacking midfield. He loved his new creative, playmaker role just behind Dirk and Fernando. As the 2008–9 season progressed, the team got better and better.

'This is going to be our year!' Jamie screamed with joy, after Liverpool had just thrashed league leaders

Manchester United 4-1 at Old Trafford.

They kept winning match after match but, unfortunately, so did United, and Liverpool finished the season four points behind their rivals.

'We came so close!' Jamie groaned. Second place was good but not quite good enough. In everything he did, Jamie always wanted to finish first.

'We'll come back and win it next season!' the Liverpool players agreed, but that next season got off to a terrible start.

For years, their defence had been one of the best in the Premiership. Jamie was so proud of their clean sheet records but, suddenly, Liverpool were conceding lots of goals. The new defenders weren't communicating with each other. The team's strong sense of organisation was gone. They were all over the place.

'My ball!' Jamie shouted but his new centre-back partner Martin Škrtel didn't hear him. He went for the ball too and they clashed heads in the air.

'We've got a lot of work to do,' Jamie thought to himself as he ran back on to the field with a bandage wrapped around his head.

For the first time since 2004, he was in danger of losing his place in the Liverpool starting line-up. Some of the supporters argued that Jamie had become a weak link in defence because he was too clumsy and slow. He was devastated.

'How can they say that after everything I've done for this club?' he asked Rafa.

'Football fans have short memories,' the Liverpool manager reminded him. 'You've got to keep fighting and come back stronger.'

Jamie was determined to prove his doubters wrong. There was no way that he was finished yet. When Manchester United visited Anfield, Daniel was back at Jamie's side. Together, they were ready to stop Wayne Rooney and Dimitar Berbatov.

'Let's do our fans proud today!' Jamie shouted in the dressing room before kick-off. With Stevie missing, he was the captain again.

Jamie loved playing in Liverpool vs Manchester United matches. It was one of the biggest rivalries in English football, and the atmosphere at Anfield was always extra-special.

With the pressure on, Jamie played one of his best games in years. He marked Rooney tightly and didn't give him any space to create chances.

'Up! Up!' Jamie shouted to his fellow defenders, organising them in a straight line across the pitch.

They formed a solid wall that the Manchester United attackers just couldn't break through. At the final whistle, Liverpool were the winners and Jamie had yet another clean sheet. Rafa was delighted with his captain's performance.

'You were an absolute rock today,' the manager told him. 'After that, the fans won't be complaining for a while!'

Jamie was determined to battle until the very end of his career. When Rafa was sacked, Liverpool needed their heroic defender more than ever. Away at Tottenham, Jamie made one of his trademark blocks on his own goal-line.

'Carra to the rescue yet again!' Martin cheered.

But Jamie was struggling against the pace of Gareth Bale, Luka Modri and Jermain Defoe. As he chased after them, he fell and landed awkwardly.

Jamie felt the pain shooting through his shoulder. He was in absolute agony.

'Careful, be gentle!' the physio told him as he helped Jamie off the pitch. He was still trying to use his arm to give instructions to his teammates.

Jamie didn't want to rest but that was exactly what his body needed. He had played over fifty matches for six seasons in a row. Even warriors couldn't keep going forever.

'You're an old man now!' his wife Nicola teased him but it was true.

When he returned to the Liverpool team, Jamie played fewer games. New manager Brendan Rodgers, who arrived in 2012, saved him for the most important matches. Jamie loved the big battles but he wasn't sure how much longer he could last at the top level.

'I want to stop while I'm still playing well,' he told Stevie. 'I've had an amazing career and I'm going to keep it that way!'

On 7 February 2013, after months of thinking, Jamie made his big announcement. He would be retiring at the end of the season.

'It has been a privilege and an honour to represent this great club for as long as I have,' he told the fans.

During seventeen seasons at Liverpool, Jamie had won three League Cups, two FA Cups, the UEFA Cup and the Champions League. But perhaps best of all, Jamie had become a Liverpool legend. There were certainly more talented footballers that had played for the club but no-one had played with more courage and passion. In whatever position he played, Jamie gave everything for the team and the Liverpool fans loved him for that. There would only ever be one 'Carra', the Boy from Bootle.

Turn the page for a sneak preview of
another brilliant football story by
Matt and Tom Oldfield. . .

STEVEN GERRARD

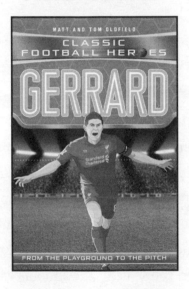

Available now!

CHAPTER 1

ANFIELD FAREWELL

16 May 2015

It was a sunny afternoon as the two teams walked out at Anfield, Liverpool in red and Crystal Palace in yellow. On the pitch, the players lined up opposite each other to form a tunnel. Liverpool only had ten – there was one very important player still to come.

'Ladies and gentlemen,' the announcer began. 'This club has been privileged to have many fantastic footballers putting on the red shirt over the years but this player, this man, is truly unique. Please raise your cards now to welcome your captain on to the pitch for his final game at Anfield, the one and only STEVIE GERRARD!'

Everyone in the stadium clapped and cheered as Stevie walked on with his three daughters, Lilly-Ella, Lexie and Lourdes. As he moved down the line, the Crystal Palace players gave him high-fives. They had so much respect for all that Stevie had achieved.

Around the centre circle, Stevie waved to all of the fans who had helped to make his Liverpool career so special. He would never forget them, just as they would never forget him. In front of him, at the Kop end, was the most amazing thing he'd ever seen. There were lots of flags showing his name and face, and the fans were holding up cards that spelt out 'SG' in huge letters with the number '8' in the middle. Along the side of the pitch, the cards spelt out 'CAPTAIN'. The fans sang his chants again and again.

Steve Gerrard, Gerrard
He'll pass the ball forty yards
He shoots the ball really hard
Steve Gerrard, Gerrard

Stevie Gerrard is our captain,
Stevie Gerrard is a red;
Stevie Gerrard plays for Liverpool,
A Scouser born and bred.

Stevie had to fight back tears as he got ready for kick-off. The club meant so much to him but after seventeen seasons, it was time to leave Liverpool. He had touched the iconic 'This is Anfield' sign outside the dressing room for the last time as a Liverpool player and captain.

The Liverpool supporters sang 'You'll Never Walk Alone' at the tops of their voices. Stevie would always get goosebumps when he heard the club anthem. The team was desperate to get a final win for Stevie and when Adam Lallana scored the opening goal, he ran to give Stevie a big hug. 'That was for you!' he said.

But Crystal Palace weren't interested in giving Stevie a happy ending to his Liverpool story. They scored two goals and suddenly Liverpool were risking defeat.

'I can be the hero one last time,' Stevie said to himself. 'I really want to score!'

He felt tired after another long season and every shot he took went wide of the goal. The fans called for him to keep shooting but in the last minute, Palace made it 3–1.

It was disappointing to end a club career with a defeat but it wasn't really about the result. It was about a captain saying goodbye to his supporters, and the supporters saying goodbye to their captain.

The Liverpool players came back out on to the pitch wearing '8 GERRARD' T-shirts.

'A whole team of Gerrards would be amazing!' Martin Škrtel joked with his teammates. 'We would definitely win the Premier League!'

As Stevie walked out, the singing started all over again. He waved to his wife, Alex, and his parents, Paul Sr and Julie, in the crowd. Without their love and strength, he couldn't have become such a superstar. The club presented him with a trophy in the shape of the Number '8' and then it was time for Stevie to speak. He had been dreading this moment for weeks. It was one thing scoring goals in front of 44,000 people but speaking was very different. He was very nervous but with Lourdes in his arms, he took the microphone.

'I am going to miss this so much,' he said, looking up into the stands. 'I'm devastated that I'll never play in front of these supporters again.'

Stevie thanked everyone at Liverpool: all of the coaches and managers he had played under and all of the teammates that he had played with. He was so grateful to everyone for all of their support over the years.

'I've played in front of a lot of supporters around the world but you're the best,' he concluded. 'Thank you very much.'

It didn't feel real – was he really leaving Liverpool? When he was young, Stevie never thought that he would leave his beloved club. Top teams had tried to sign him but he had stayed loyal. It wasn't about money; it was about love and pride. Now he was off to play in the USA, for a new club in a new league – but nothing would ever compare to Liverpool.

He had played 709 games, 503 in the Premier League, and he had scored 119 goals. With his team, he had won the Champions League, the UEFA Cup, the FA Cup twice and the League Cup three times. He had so many amazing memories from his time at Anfield. It was here that he had grown up from a fierce-tackling skinny kid to become a world-class, goalscoring midfielder and the captain of club and country.

It had been an amazing journey for this young Liverpool fan from Huyton, and Stevie had loved every minute of it.

JAMIE CARRAGHER HONOURS

Juventus

🏆 UEFA Cup: 2000-01

🏆 FA Cup: 2000–01, 2005–06

🏆 UEFA Super Cup: 2001, 2005

🏆 League Cup: 2000–01, 2002–03, 2011–12

🏆 UEFA Champions League: 2004–05

Individual

🏆 Liverpool Player of the Year Award: 1999, 2005, 2007

🏆 PFA Team of the Year: 2006

CARRAGHER

㉓ THE FACTS

NAME: Jamie Lee Duncan Carragher

DATE OF BIRTH: 28 January 1978

AGE: 39

PLACE OF BIRTH: Bootle, Merseyside

NATIONALITY: England

BEST FRIEND: Steven Gerrard

CURRENT CLUB: Liverpool

POSITION: CB

THE STATS

Height (cm):	183
Club appearances:	737
Club goals:	4
Club trophies:	11
International appearances:	38
International goals:	0
International trophies:	0
Ballon d'Ors:	0

★ ★ ★ **HERO RATING: 85** ★ ★ ★

GREATEST MOMENTS

Type and search the web links to see the magic for yourself!

1 17 MAY 1996, LIVERPOOL 2-1 WEST HAM

https://www.youtube.com/watch?v=Ej57BGsLr8E

Jamie had already moved position from striker to midfielder but in the 1996 FA Youth Cup Final, he became the defender that we know and love. Michael Owen was Liverpool's goal scoring hero but Jamie was their hero at the back. As always, he gave 110 per cent for his team and made lots of great blocks and tackles.

18 JANUARY 1997,
LIVERPOOL 3-0 ASTON VILLA

https://www.youtube.com/watch?v=S7gupDRNAAA

As long as he was in the team, Jamie was happy to play anywhere on the pitch for Liverpool. In just his second Premier League match, he played in central midfield against Aston Villa's Andy Townsend. He did well and in the second-half, he scored a header from a corner! It was the first of only four goals in 737 appearances.

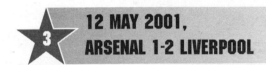

12 MAY 2001,
ARSENAL 1-2 LIVERPOOL

https://www.youtube.com/watch?v=qmEh9k70g9A

In the 2001 FA Cup Final, Liverpool faced an Arsenal team featuring Dennis Bergkamp, Patrick Vieira and Thierry Henry. In an epic battle, The Reds came out victorious, thanks to Michael Owen's goals and the heroic defending of Jamie and Sami Hyypiä. Liverpool won The Treble that season: the League Cup, the FA Cup and the UEFA Cup.

25 MAY 2005, LIVERPOOL 3-3 AC MILAN (3-2 ON PENALTIES)

https://www.youtube.com/watch?v=ubK8A-yfm3w
Throughout this incredible Champions League
Final, Steven Gerrard was Liverpool's star attacker
and Jamie was Liverpool's star defender. Despite
exhaustion and bad cramp in his leg, he kept
going and made tackle after tackle. This was the
performance that made Jamie a true Liverpool legend.

19 MAY 2013, LIVERPOOL 1-0 QPR

https://www.youtube.com/watch?v=Xdhc8VD5SQ4
After seventeen seasons of great performances, Jamie
said goodbye to professional football at Anfield. The
players formed a guard of honour and the fans sang his
song - 'We All Dream of a Team of Carraghers'. It was
a special moment for Jamie, who had made the second
most appearances in Liverpool history. He finished in
style, with a win and yet another clean sheet.

PLAY LIKE YOUR HEROES

THE JAMIE CARRAGHER
SLIDING BLOCK

SEE IT HERE **You Tube**

https://www.youtube.com/watch?v=o_3sUKACl0c

STEP 1: Always be alert to potential danger.

STEP 2: When the ball is played up to the striker, run across to block his path to goal. You're going to do everything possible to stop him scoring.

STEP 3: If the striker is outside the penalty area, don't dive in straight away. Use your football experience to choose the right moment.

STEP 4: But if the striker is already inside the penalty area, don't delay. It's time to slide!

STEP 5: Throw yourself to the floor, with your right leg stretched out. You want to make yourself as big as possible.

STEP 6: Be totally fearless.

STEP 7: Get back up quickly and start shouting at your teammates again!

TEST YOUR KNOWLEDGE

QUESTIONS

1. What's the name of the local team where Jamie played and his dad coached?

2. Who was Jamie's first football hero?

3. Jamie's first club was Everton – true or false?

4. Which famous Italian goalkeeper did Jamie score against while playing at Lilleshall?

5. Back at Liverpool, Jamie moved back into midfield to make way for which young striker?

6. Why did Jamie play in defence in the Youth Cup Final?

7. Which team did Jamie score his first senior Liverpool goal against?

8. Who were the four members of Liverpool's defence when they won the Treble in 2001?

9. Which Liverpool manager helped Jamie to become a world-class centre-back?

10. What position did Jamie play for England in the 2006 World Cup?

11. How many cup finals did Jamie win at the Millennium Stadium in Cardiff?

Answers below. . . No cheating!

1. Merton Villa 2. Everton striker Graeme Sharp 3. False – he did join Everton for a short period when he was 11 but he soon went back to Liverpool 4. Gianluigi Buffon 5. Michael Owen 6. Liverpool's centre-back, Eddie Turkington, was suspended. 7. Aston Villa 8. Markus Babbel at right-back, Sami Hyypiä and Stéphane Henchoz in the middle, and Jamie at left-back. 9. Rafa Benítez 10. Right-back 11. Four – 2001 League Cup, 2001 FA Cup, 2003 League Cup and 2006 FA Cup

HAVE YOU GOT THEM ALL?

ULTIMATE FOOTBALL HEROES